ENGLISH LANGUAGE
IN INDIA

ENGLISH LANGUAGE IN INDIA

Dr Rachel K Daniel

GYAN

Published, 2019

Published by

Gyan Publishing House
5, Ansari Road
Daryaganj, New Delhi-110002
Phone: 011-47034999, 9811692060
www.gyanbooks.com
E-mail: books@gyanbooks.com

Printed at: G. Print Process, Delhi.

Cataloging in Publication Data—DK
Courtesy: D.K. Agencies (P) Ltd. <docinfo@dkagencies.com>

Daniel, Rachel K., author.
English language in India / Dr Rachel K Daniel.
pages cm
ISBN 9788121214919

1. English language—India—History. I. Title.

LCC PE3502.I6D36 2019 | DDC 420.954 23

Contents

Preface

English is the most successful language in the history of the world. English as a Lingua Franca is accepted today as an ideology in language and it is thriving and growing vibrantly across nations and cultures. There are a number of factors influencing and developing English as the lingua franca. Worldwide, non-native speakers of English outnumber native speakers; they also vary from standard of English due to various cultural contexts not traditionally associated with the language. In India a total of around 400 million people use English, more than the combined English speaking population of the first language countries. Moreover, English is learnt as a second language by millions in India. It has a special regional status in India and is an important unifying medium between the Indo-European North and the Dravidian South. India has a unique position in the English speaking world. It is a linguistic bridge between the major first language dialects of the world, such as British and American English and other major foreign language varieties emerging in China and Japan.

The English spoken in India is different from that spoken in other regions of the world. It is regarded as a unique variety which is called Indian English. It might be difficult for the native speaker of English to digest the fact that currently India is in its pathway towards becoming the largest English speaking nation in the world. English has changed Indian languages in many ways, mostly through the incorporation of new words. The purpose of this book has been to prove how this massive foreign language growth has evolved and what factors and issues have influenced and affected this transformation. The global spread of English may also be associated with decreased use of endangered languages. The future of English is in the hands of countries outside the core of Anglophone group. Is English going to be learnt for ever or not is an unanswerable question that only time will answer.

Foreword

I have had the privilege of being one of the supervisors of the PhD thesis from which this book emerged, so am well acquainted with the depth of knowledge and understanding that Dr Rachel Daniel, as author, brings to this informative text. As an academic straddling life, work and research in Australia and India, the author brings a set of unique insights into the topic which ultimately broadens the appeal of her research. While I have personally supervised many doctoral projects, I found that this study of the growth of the English language in India to be particularly interesting and pertinent in the context of the increasingly globalised world in which we live. It is heartening that the results of this research can now be made available to the broader public through this publication.

The book takes the reader on a journey that includes an impressive account of the extent of English language usage in India before expanding to a broader view of English as the Lingua Franca due to its potential as the language of international communication. While the author offers a concise but representative account of the research process that underpinned the project behind this book, she manages to present the methodology and research findings in a manner that opens it up to those outside the world of academe. The carefully chosen focus on specific aspects of the doctoral thesis is evident in the three chapters that are dedicated to the research process, namely Chapters 4, 5 and 6. These chapters highlight specific aspects of Dr Daniel's findings that illustrate her argument in Chapter 1, that the use of English in India has grown so significantly over the past five decades, that it has become the "de facto national language of India".

However, as is so aptly pointed out by Dr Daniel, the growing use of English in India is not an uncontested space, due to concomitant concerns about the possibility of languages and dialects dying out in response. This aspect has not been shied away from in the book, with the author tackling the issue in the final chapter, consoling readers that "the sheer number of speakers of India's native languages more or less ensures that they do not face extinction". The final chapter is possibly the most important one in the book in terms of providing insights into tensions associated with the range of possible future directions for the use of the English language in India. In fact, Dr Daniel concludes her book with a discussion of the swift rise of globalisation and the concomitant benefits associated with being well prepared to make the most of this opening up of the world. In educational terms, she explains how "Support in developing the knowledge and skills of local students about global processes both by embedding them in core curriculum and in providing co-curricular opportunities to learn emphatic communication life skills with English language acquisition will see Indians develop further as a formidable nation and power house in the global sphere".

Overall, I believe that *English Language in India* is a valuable and timely resource for anyone wishing to gain a better understanding of how the English language has come to be used by "more than 125 million Indians" and is "spreading throughout the world far more rapidly than any other language". I think this book provides important information and perspectives to help guide readers understanding of this phenomenon in a way that has not been presented before.

As an educator in our increasingly globalised world, I commend this book to you.

Assoc Prof Margaret Plunkett
School of Education
Federation University, Australia

Acknowledgement

English as a Lingua Franca is today an accepted ideology in language and it is thriving and growing vibrantly across nations and cultures. In the meantime, it is raising a considerable debate in linguistics on its directions and where the rest of the languages of the world are going to. With the unprecedented diffusion of education across the globe, the vast English language dispersion has substantially increased since the post- colonial period in India. Moreover, around 125,000,000 people use English in India which is more than the combined English speaking population of the first language countries. A comprehensive study to investigate the factors influencing English language growth in India was the main objective envisaged for the research. The Ph.D research was conducted at Monash University, Victoria, Australia on the topic 'India and the English Language' under the supervision of Prof. Tony Taylor and Associate Professor Margaret Plunkett.

This research investigated and tried to understand how the phenomenal growth of English language has evolved and to comprehend why it is occurring and what are the major factors influencing English language growth in India. A projection on the Future of English language in India is also presented. Appreciation is due to: Dr. P. Sam Daniel, Mr. John D. Kesari, Dr. Aroma G Sam, Dr. R.D.Sathiya, Mr. Michael Barrow and Mr. G. Natarajan for their considerable editing, reviewing and formatting of the book.

Chapter - 1

Introduction

The British Council (2013) statistics claims that the English language enjoys official or special status in at least 75 of the world's countries and for a total population of over two billion people. It is spoken as a first-language by around three hundred and seventy five million people and as a second-language by another three hundred and seventy five million speakers. There are also millions of people using English as a foreign language. It is believed that speakers of English as a second-language probably outnumber those who speak it as a first- language (Crystal, 1997). Around 900 million people are believed to be using English as a foreign language. One out of four in the world's population speaks English to some level of competence.

Worldwide, non-native speakers of English out number native speakers, they also vary from forms of English for cultural contexts not traditionally associated with the language. Particular groups of English speakers who could be native or non-native, cannot therefore be acquainted with more than a subset of the language patterns and conventions developed during this broad diversification of English usage (Mesthrie, 2008). With the unprecedented diffusion of education, the core of the English-knowing and English-using population has substantially increased during the post-colonial period. All social classes are now keen to learn English at some level and have access to some kind of English instruction.

Of India's population of over 1.3 billion (indiastat.com, 2012) about 3 percent are competent in using English language. Globalization and urbanization in India have brought rapid changes which have pushed the total much higher, to about 5 percent (Lewis, 2009). The main reasons for this have been the opportunities for outsourcing, use of English as a second-language in all the seven states of the North-East India and the growing urban population that became cosmopolitan. The Indian subcontinent comprising Bangladesh, Pakistan, Sri Lanka, Nepal and Bhutan provides a broader population estimate of English usage. As of 2012 it is believed that around nine hundred to a thousand million inhabitants live in countries where English is an associate official language (Nation Master, 2012).

It is now almost impossible for people to fully participate in the global village that they live in without 'knowing' a common world language. In fact, new linguistic insights have shown that no human language is superior to any other and that the development and growth of a language depend upon its use (Sarwal, 2011). Moreover languages cannot have any independent existence since it solely exists in the brain, mouth, ears, hands and eyes of the user, than on any mystical space or even literary form. Meanwhile, English, for various reasons primarily due to British rule in the many parts of the world has emerged as the popular lingua franca. In the process, it must be acknowledged, the role of English and its functions have vastly changed. English is no longer seen as the language of rulers, or as an instrument for promoting British culture and values. Tom McArthur, (2003), the famous linguist in his introduction to *The Oxford Companion to the English Language* claims that it has been towards the very end of the twentieth century that the English language has become a global resource. Hence it cannot be claimed that it does not owe its very existence, patronage or the defense of its very nature and uniqueness to any nation or group.

Regional languages issue still provide a platform for political activists in several states. Regional language politics are sometimes aimed at Hindi, sometimes at English, and sometimes at migrant or minority communities. India is home to many languages, and its constitution, education system and working practices recognise this. Education systems tend to value only some languages and may attempt to eradicate the variety and fluidity in language use that children bring to school. This is one of the ways in which education encourages language loss. English is in greater demand in India than ever before as parents and employers want it, and public policy increasingly accepts the need to provide universal access to it. On the other hand, how can opportunities for learning English be provided efficiently and effectively in such a diverse and dynamic environment. In response to a rising demand from parents for English medium education today, education authorities across India are introducing more English into government schools. Arguments about the medium of schooling have run for many years, often spilling into the law courts. The belief and trend that an English education leads to higher education and better jobs is predominantly true, and it is seen by lower castes as an escape route from social imprisonment. Across the cross section of India, English medium education is believed to work to disperse educational outcomes. For a small minority, it results in better English skills but no better general educational outcomes. This small minority, who have an "English friendly" environment, an English medium education poses no hurdle, or a very small one. But the rewards are linked to opportunities in the global marketplace for higher education and jobs, including the export oriented service industries in India. However, for the large majority, English medium education works differently, leading to poorer educational outcomes and poorer language skills, and this is a matter of great concern to education administrators.

The higher education system in India has grown in a remarkable way, particularly in the post independence period, to become one of the largest systems of its kind in the world. However, the system faces many difficulties at present: financing and management concerns, including access, equity and relevance; a needed reorientation of programs, laying emphasis on health consciousness, values and ethics; a need to establish quality standards of higher education by reviewing the assessment of institutions and their accreditation. These issues are important for the country, as it is now engaged in the use of higher education as a powerful tool to build a knowledge based information society of the 21st century. Universities have to perform multiple roles, creating new knowledge, acquiring new capabilities and producing an intelligent human resource pool; they must accomplish this through challenging teaching, research and extension activities so as to balance both the need and the demand. Recognizing and achieving these goals is a very high undertaking for the planners and implementers of education policy in India.

Efficient teacher supply is another recurrent problem in developing countries, especially where the population is growing rapidly. The pool of educated adults is small in comparison to the large numbers of children who need to be taught. English teachers tend to be in especially short supply. Anyone who can speak English can usually find a much better paid job elsewhere in the economy, making both recruitment and retention of English teachers difficult, particularly in rural areas. Currently employed English teachers who have spent their careers teaching grammar and literature may not have the skills to teach spoken English, at this moment regarded as the starting point for most English curriculums. Increasing the amount of English in the curriculum is typically a part of wider educational reforms, and teachers of other subjects need to be redeployed to undertake this. Labour laws may be needed that will require otherwise redundant teachers to be retrained as English teachers. In addition, teaching English to young learners presents a special challenge since teachers of younger age groups often have a lower level of education than secondary teachers, and are least likely to have good English language skills. Several of India's challenges with regard to English language education are not exclusive but very similar to the experiences of other developing countries. What makes India unique is the combination of size and complexity. China is the only other developing country which can match India for size in both population and economy, however it has a completely different language situation in that it lacks a colonial legacy in relation to English, excluding Hong Kong, and educational decisions are taken in a different political context.

India is often spoken of as a great power in the same breath as China because of its billion plus population, economic promise, value as a trading partner and growing military capabilities. This is seen as a misconception by many as there are very few similarities between the two Asian giants. As forecasted by The Economist (2013) "Although poorer and less economically dynamic than China, India has soft power in abundance. It is committed to democratic institutions, the rule of law and human rights. As a victim of jihadist violence, it is in the front rank of the fight against terrorism. It has a huge and talented Diaspora. It may not want to be coopted by the West, but it shares many western values. It is confident and culturally rich. India is well placed to provide security in a critical part of the global commons. That India can become a great power is not in doubt. The real question is whether it wants to".

One of the main challenges facing many countries is how to maintain their identity in the face of globalization and growing multilingualism. There is a case for regulating the status of English but ways need to be found of reinventing nation's identity around a distinctive mix rather than a single language which is kept pure. The need to protect the national languages, and scheduled languages in India is to ensure that English does not intrude or unnecessarily take over too many domains. Public communication, pedagogic and formal genres and new modes of communication facilitated by technology, may be key domains to defend (Graddol, 2006). The global spread of English may also be associated with decreased use of endangered languages.

English has changed Indian languages in many ways, mostly through the incorporation of new words. However, the population of English speakers in India, though socially influential, remains a small minority. Also, most of these individuals are conversant in at least one, if not two or three, other languages, and unless the situation necessitates English, they usually speak in their native language. It seems that multiple languages can function together when they each have their particular domains of use (Baldridge, 2002). The sheer number of speakers of India's native languages more or less ensures that they do not face extinction.

English is still in a slightly precarious position. Although it has a strong base in the elite class of India and in the general culture, it could easily fall victim to an anti-English movement if one ever arises. Public fervor is known to be especially forceful in India, and a skillful leader could use it to create such a movement. Hopefully, this will not happen. Indians have a lot to gain from knowing English, and the world has a lot to gain from Indians knowing English. Some Indians complain that English brings in too much western thought, but English in India also exports a vast amount of Indian culture and thought to the rest of the world. This will increase the diversity of experience that people around the world receive as part of their education.

Chapter - 2

English Language: A Profile

Language Issues in India

English is the most successful language in the history of the world. It is spoken on every continent, is learnt as a second language by school children and is the vehicle of science, global business and popular culture. It is predicted to continue to spread without borders because conquest, trade and religion were the biggest forces behind the spread of earlier lingua Francas. However, English as a Lingua Franca is today an accepted ideology in language and it is thriving and growing vibrantly across nations and cultures while raising a considerable debate in linguistics on its directions and where the rest of the languages of the world are going to. The English language today has various proposes depending on the context it is being used and what the ultimate aim of learning the language is going to serve.

English is expanding as a lingua Franca but not as a mother tongue. Through the last five decades, English has become the de facto national language of India. Almost all advertising billboards in India are in English. There is not a single well-paying job in the country that does not require a good understanding of the language while higher education is conducted entirely in English. Since independence, the influence and reach of English have grown immensely. It is impossible to arrive at a credible figure for the number of Indians who understand English or on who can read it and who can write it. On the other hand, what is indisputable is that in India today, English has the force and quality of a national language. English is predicted to remain the dominant language in the world and is expected to continue to grow in India in the foreseeable future because Hindi is not accepted as a uniting national language in India and nor Mandarin in the world in spite of the growth in the Chinese population. Further more, the number of English speakers in China are already growing more rapidly than the number of Mandarin speakers, especially among the youth as the population explodes in the two most populous nations in the world. India already has more than 125 million English speakers and it's likely this number will continue to expand along with the population and by just focusing on demographic trends alone English will remain the world's most widely spoken language.

It is difficult making predictions about languages but one certainty is that languages change as time passes on. Who could have guessed that two thousand years after its Golden Age Latin would have ceased to be a living language, unused and almost extinct (Clackson, Horrocks, &Library, 2011). Sanskrit and Greek lost their position as living languages. There is a need for caution, then, when we seek to predict the future formal character of English. For example, since foreign learners of English have difficulty in pronouncing inter dental fricatives(as in thin, this), it may not be surprising to see them disappear completely within the next fifty years; they have already disappeared from some accents, such as Cockney and Iris. In grammar, a number of terms are accepted in second or foreign language situations that today's Standard English would reject as 'un-English', but' information", for example, was Standard English term once: an "information" and an "information" can be traced back to Middle English, and are found in Chaucer, Shakespeare, Swift and many other writers. It may only be a matter of time before they are back (Crystal, 2008).

English is spreading throughout the world far more rapidly than any other language. This has much less to do with a sentimental attachment to, or genuine liking for, English than with a necessity-based desire to learn it. Graddol (1996) foresees that there is a possibility that the spread of English is slowing relative to other languages as rapid economic and military changes around the world weaken people's need to learn it. In many countries too, local authorities are engaged in language-planning to affirm and strengthen the use of their national language so that it continues to serve many functions for their people while simultaneously fostering the spread of English as a link language. It is a difficult set of companion goals when the goal of learning English makes the rest of the world increasingly bilingual or multilingual; the Anglophone world remains predominantly monolingual. The fact that its level of functional bilingual is very low is expected to have a negative impact on the spread and survival of English in the long run (Quirk, 1968).

Ostler (2010) a scholar of the rise and fall of languages, makes a surprising prediction that the days of English as the world's lingua franca may be numbered. Conquest, trade and religion were the biggest forces behind the spread of earlier lingua Francas. Many civilizations and their languages have been vanquished in history. The Babylonians in 539 BC, spoke Persian as their native language, but pragmatically adopted Aramaic the mother tongue of Jesus Christ as the world's first "interlingua" (Paul,2012).Official long-distance communications were written in Aramaic, sent across the empire and then translated. Persian itself would serve as a lingua Franca, not at the time of the empire's greatest heights but roughly from 1000 AD to 1800 AD. Persian was also the court language of the Mogul kings who had been ruling Mugal India when the British East India Company arrived (Ostler, 2010).

Moreover, the core arguments about the future of English by Ostler (2010) are striking. English is expanding as a lingua franca but not as a mother tongue. More than a billion people speak English worldwide but only about 330 million of them as a first-language and this population is not spreading. The future of English is in the hands of countries outside the core Anglophone group. Is English going to be learnt for ever or not is an unanswerable question that only time will answer (The Economist, 2013).

The factors that will check the spread of English are modern nationalist and technological development and Ostler (2010) concurs. Several of Britain's ex-colonies accepted English as the lingua franca only because English was an cultural language among competing native tongues. Nevertheless, English has been rejected in other ex-colonies while in countries like Sri Lanka and Tanzania Anglophone elites gave way to Sinhala and Swahili speaking nationalists (The Economist, 2013). Ostler (2010) argues that English will have no successor because none will be needed. Technology will fill the need. The argument relies on huge advances in computer translation and speech recognition. Nationalist limits to the spread of English as a mother-tongue and technological developments will replace the spread of English and hence it may become something like calligraphy or Latin, prestigious and traditional, but increasingly dispersible (The Economist, 2013).

English has a polymorphous nature (Jenkins, 2009) which has aided it through the centuries to evolve, adapt and flourish in diverse environments through acceptance, integration and tolerance. There are many factors influencing and developing English as the lingua franca of the world as Global English is making it universally usable. That is, English is being spoken by people in the most number of countries around the world. This research endeavoured to identify through surveys and interviews some of the major factors influencing the growth of English in the Indian subcontinent and understand the perceptions of educators across disciplines and age groups.

How many people speak English in India?

The British Council (2013) statistics claims that the English language enjoys official or special status in at least 75 of the world's countries and for a total population of over two billion people. It is spoken as a first-language by around three hundred and seventy five million people and as a second-language by another three hundred and seventy five million speakers. There are also millions of people using English as a foreign language. It is believed that speakers of English as a second-language probably outnumber those who speak it as a firstlanguage (Crystal, 1997). Around 900 million people are believed to be using English as a foreign language. One out of four in the world's population speaks English to some level of competence.

Worldwide, non-native speakers of English out number native speakers, they also vary from forms of English for cultural contexts not traditionally associated with the language. Particular groups of English speakers who could be native or non-native, cannot therefore be acquainted with more than a subset of the language patterns and conventions developed during this broad diversification of English usage (Mesthrie, 2008). With the unprecedented diffusion of education, the core of the English-knowing and English-using population has substantially increased during the post-colonial period. All social classes are now keen to learn English at some level and have access to some kind of English instruction.

How Many Use English in the Indian Subcontinent?

Of India's population of over 1.3 billion (indiastat.com, 2012) about 3 percent are competent in using English language. Globalization and urbanization in India have brought rapid changes which have pushed the total much higher, to about 5 percent (Lewis, 2009). The main reasons for this have been the opportunities for outsourcing, use of English as a second-language in all the seven states of the North-East India and the growing urban population that became cosmopolitan. The Indian subcontinent comprising Bangladesh, Pakistan, Sri Lanka, Nepal and Bhutan provides a broader population estimate of English usage. As of 2012 it is believed that around nine hundred to a thousand million inhabitants live in countries where English is an associate official language (Nation Master, 2012).

Kachru, Kachru, and Nelson (2006) point out that English is the language of the legal system, a major language in parliament and a preferred language in the universities. The All-India Competitive Examinations for senior administrative, engineering and foreign service positions require English skills that demonstrate competence, 'educated awareness' or 'fluent command'. Meanwhile the spread of semi-fluent and 'broken' English encountered in the Indian subcontinent amongst people of limited educational background is remarkable in its extent. In India a total of around 400 million people use English, more than the combined English-speaking population of the first- language countries (indiastat.com, 2013). There are no better thoroughly researched, studied and analysed authorities on theories, figures and data about English in India other than Crystal (1997) and Graddol (1997) whose statistical information might be observed to be a few decades old, but is thorough, comprehensive and reliable as recommended by the world authority on the English language the British Council (2013).

Estimates for second language and foreign language competence reinforce the point that has been made with increasing emphasis over the past decade that the centre of gravity of the English language has moved away from the native speaker: there are now three or four nonnative speakers for one native speaker, a ratio that will increase as time goes by (Graddol, 1997). Indian English, however, varies from Britishor American English, as it has been influenced by indigenous linguistics through the years. With an English-speaking population surpassing that of the UK and the US combined, and using a dynamic variety of English, India is set to become a linguistic superpower, (Crystal,2004).

Moreover, English is learned as a second language by millions. It has a special regional status in India and is an important unifying medium between the Indo-European North and the Dravidian South. Its influence permeates daily life for many. Unquestionably, as it spreads throughout the country Indian English is changing quite fast and in an unique fashion. India's cultural and linguistic diversity are major factors in this change with incoming English usages filtering through regional dialects and local language patterns. To some extent Indian English is having trouble distancing itself from the weigh to fits British past with some inclined to think of Indian English as inferior to British English. At the same time a fresh confidence is emerging among the youth, and it seems only a matter of time before such attitudes change (Crystal,2004).

In addition, India has a unique position in the English speaking world. It is a linguistic bridge between the major first- language dialects of the world, such as British and American English, and other major foreign language varieties emerging in China and Japan (Crystal, 2004). Indian English has a special status and the linguistic status of any language in a nation is always a reflection of power that is also political, economic, technological, cultural and religious. This is clearly the case in India where tremendous cyber-technological progress and the growth of Indian English are together galvanising the economy and transforming the face of Indian society. To cite just one example, the call centre phenomenon has stimulated a huge expansion of internet related activity. Currently the amount of text English messaging (SMS) in India exceeds that of the UK and the US. Moreover many in the IT press speculate that the future base of Google operations will one day be India (Crystal, 2004).

Varieties of English

The English spoken in India is different from that spoken in other regions of the world. It is regarded as a unique variety which is called Indian English. Many Indians claim that it is very similar to British English, but this opinion is based on a superficial examination of lexical similarities. In reality, a great deal of regional and educational differentiations exists at various phonological, morphological, lexical and syntactic levels (Deterding, 2011). When one discusses 'World Englishes', an analysis of Tom McArthur's (2003) Circle of World English (Figure 1) and Kachru's (1983) model of World English (Figure 2 gives a wider perspective of the varieties of English.

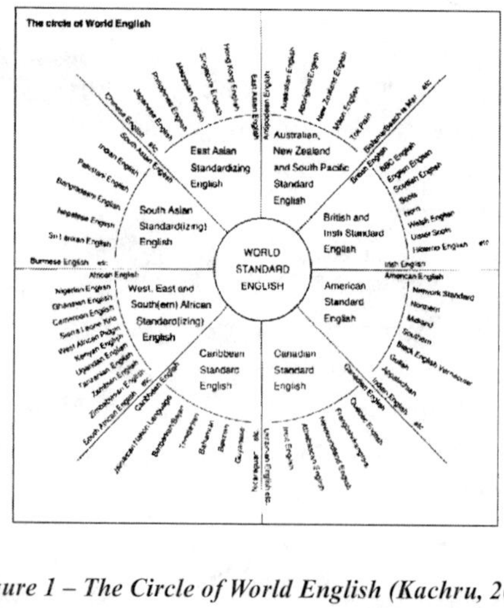

Figure 1 – The Circle of World English (Kachru, 2001)

The spread of English may be viewed in terms of three concentric circles. The Inner circle, the Outer (or Extended) circle and the Extending circle. These circles represent the types of spread, the patterns of acquisition, the range of functional domains, and the societal penetration of the language.

THE INNER CIRCLE USA
242,200,000
UK 56,458,000
Canada 25,625,000

THE OUTER (or Extended)
CIRCLEe.g

Bangladesh 104,204,000
Ghana 13,552,000
India 783,940,000
Kenya 21,044,000
Malaysia 15,820,000
Nigeria 105,448,000

THE EXTENDING CIRCLE e.g
Bangladesh 104,204,000
Ghana 13,552,000
India 783,940,000
Kenya 21,044,000
Malaysia 15,820,000
Nigeria 105,448,000

Figure 2 – Three Concentric Circles of English (Kachru,2001)

Estimates about total users of English: 350 million native

Conservative:	400 million non-native
Optimistic:	2 billion

McArthur's (2003) Circle of World English is comprehensive and covers most of the Varieties of English whereas Kachru's (1983) Model of World English fails to include South African English, in particular, and some other African, European varieties and Caribbean varieties. Masthrie (2008) states that Kachru's (1983) model avoids mention of South Africa where English had a sizable mother tongue presence in the1980s.

A particular challenge for English in education in the 21st Century is in understanding and developing the appropriate methodologies on how to equip young native speakers of English with open flexible ways of communicating in a pluralingual culture while also developing their own richly expressive personal forms or styles (Davidson, 2007). However our modern highly technology oriented new generation of youth might develop solutions of their own in their evolutionary process which will have to be adopted and will be as time and technology move on.

Indian English

It is generally accepted that English acquired its global status as a consequence of the economic domination achieved by the Englishspeaking world. As a result, the lingua franca of India is English, the working, unifying language of this vast multilingual nation. Under the impact of globalization and economic rationalism, English is increasingly competing with the indigenous languages (Krishnasamy, 2007).As might be expected, Indian English is constantly changing.

An inevitable consequence of this huge country's cultural and linguistic diversity is a continual flow and cross flow of influence between regional dialects. Indubitably the noticeable differences of regional accent and dialect remain, especially between North and South Indian English. Correspondingly, even three generations after independence, Indian English is still having trouble distancing itself from the weight of British English.

History behind English in India

Even though India had won independence from British in 1947, the English language had remained a part of the social, emotional and intellectual heritage of a post-colonial India. English had been the official language of India since 1835. However, the newly formed Constituent Assembly of India began to consider the question of the official language of the country. It was decided by a majority of one vote that the official language of India would be Hindi with English continuing as an associate official language for a period of fifteen years, after which Hindi would become the sole official language. The new Constitution came into effect on 26 January 1950 (Riddick, 2006). The various states in India, originally formed on a linguistic basis were, in the new scheme of things, authorized to adopt Hindi or any other recognized Indian language for official transactions. Nevertheless, whenever the states opted to bring out bills, or acts, in any language other than English, they were required to furnish relevant translations in English. However the non- Hindi speaking states, particularly the Southern States and West Bengal, preferred the continuation of English as the official language of the country and, in the 1960s, and protested against the imposition of Hindi; these states had a genuine fear that the Hindi-speaking Northern States would have an advantage over them if Hindi became the sole official federal language. Consequently, the Official Language Amendment Act of 1967 assured to English the status of an 'Associate Official Language' without any ambiguity whatsoever until such time as the non-Hindi states should decide otherwise (Thulsi, 1983)

The prevalence of English as a common language in India is a legacy of the British who colonized the country. Surprisingly, English was not the first language to arrive on India's shores from Europe; Portuguese and Dutch had already preceded it. The arrival of the Jesuit missionaries in Goa in 1570 set the stage for the long term relationship between English and the languages of the subcontinent (Sedlatschek,2009). Throughout the world "The Age of Imperialism" was in decline following the climactic wars which progressively deprived European empires of their ability to manage their acquired overseas possessions. This rapid transformation in the international dynamics caused the subsequent transition to a new geopolitical order and a fundamentally different understanding of imperialist doctrines. The British Empire had very high principle of governance based on religion, culture and history and consequently was ordered by institutions that gave her a benevolent character compared with other conquering and colonising nations. While more aggressive imperialist nations lacked conscience, British imperialism was characterised by an original concern for the people of the nations they conquered. They worked towards spreading their political principles and free institutions across the hemispheres. British colonialism did manifest in numerable imperfections, and problems arose as they would under any foreign governance, and frequently it struggled to resolve issues; however historical records confirm "that the British Empire was one of the greatest forces for good the world had ever hosted" (Brown, 2010). Being the master of the seas and leader in industry for over two centuries had indisputably granted the nation the advantage of being supreme global power with strength at their command to control whom they wished to by its centuries long supremacy that had bred a calm authority.

The acquisition of India led to an experiment in governance on the part of Britain who had been phasing out her autocratic rule in her other colonies, however the people of India were considered unprepared for self-rule. India's maintaining accord with its British mother land's political principles was mandatory, but the size of India and the prolonged period of time London managed the subcontinent produced a test for British imperialism and showcased it at its best. The colonial era started in the 17th century when the British settled into India as traders; following a period of conquest, war and treaties, by 1858 they controlled almost the whole of India. The British had been in India, for 250 years and they had complete mastery over India for 150 years. There were about 285,000 Englishmen in India, that is, one Englishman to 1,300 Indians, until, in 1947, India gained independence after a long struggle to break free of British rule (Stanley, 1993). With the establishment of the 'India Act' in 1789 the East India Company was in full political control from Britain, with ministers in London and a Governor General in India, supervising its colony.

It can be said that because of its unwillingness to engage in acts of conquest, Great Britain was inadvertently continuing the colonisation process by immigrating to the New World, but it did not wish to commandeer control of existing civilizations. The purpose was not that the Empire should acquire this society, but a consequence of the trade wars fought between the emerging nation- states of Europe, and the rise of East India Company, was a troublesome transition from commercial enterprise to political administration (Brown, 2010). This new era of British involvement in India brought the struggle of balancing the principles of liberty with imperialism to the forefront of Parliamentary politics. Rather than acquiesce in the ways of the East, the leaders of Britain began a process and discussion over the proper role of imperial rule and the obligatory reforms of the Company apparatus (Brown, 2010).

The slow expansion and colonisation of the subcontinent meant that English language and culture only gradually influenced orthodox Indian society in the early 1600's, when the East India Company started trading and English missionaries first began their efforts at conversion. From an Indian perspective, English was initially a foreign language that had to be directly acquired from the native British English rulers, whose style set the norm. However, English Language had started to acquire loanwords from the local indigenous Indian languages (Schneider, 2003) and was largely an unstable language, frequently marked by lack of clarity at the discourse level due to the lack of formal education in English during that initial colonial period.

The process of producing English-proficient bilinguals in India began with the colonial government's "Minute of 1835", which officially endorsed the Supreme Council of India member Macaulay's goal of forming "a class who may be interpreters between us and the millions whom we govern-a class of persons, Indians in blood and colour, but English in taste, in opinion, in morals and in intellect" (Kachru, 1983, p. 22) . It is generally supposed by modern historians that the study of English was imposed upon Indians by Lord Macaulay from the Supreme Council of India which was heavily involved in redrafting the Indian penal code and in the promotion of education in India with the sole purpose of serving the colonial ends of maintaining the British administration's control of India (Riddick, 2006). Simultaneously, a large number of Christian schools imparting an English language education were set up by the early 1800's. As a result, English permeated some of the most important parts of society: the government and civil service, the media, the education system, the legal system, and gradually the social sphere as well. Following the Macaulay reforms, English became the official and academic language of India by the early twentieth century, (Baldridge, 2002). By 1882, more than sixty percent of the primary schools in the major cities were English-medium schools.

The spread of English-medium schools encouraged the use of English in a more social environment. English clubs for debating & elocution became popular forms of entertainment and extracurricular activity as the language began to evolve into the principal language of communication. Although the rising of the nationalist movement in the 1920's brought some anti-English sentiment with it, the movement itself used English as its medium (Kachru, 1994).

Sociolinguistically, Macaulay shifted the status of English from being a foreign language to becoming an official second- language .This helped the process by which a system of bilingual education spread widely in India throughout the nineteenth century. This subsequently developed elitist schooling and revolutionised the importance of the English language to be the key to social up liftment, education and political power in the society and the nation as a whole,(Schneider,2003) The position of the language continued to consolidate itself with the surge in its demand in the Indian Civil Service, Railways and other administrative spheres. The number of English-language newspapers increased and so did their readers and advertisers which resulted in the demand for editors, journalists, reporters, correspondents, printers, publishers, writers and soon. The number of English educated college students went from an estimated 36,000 students in 1911 to approximately 145,000 students by 1939 (Schneider, 2003).

Languages Spoken in India

India can be considered to be a 'Babel of languages'. The variety of languages has been built up through the ages by various races and ethnic groups that made their way into India. The major division among India's languages is between the Dravidian tongues of the South and the Indo-Aryan ones of North and Central India. The Indo-Aryan languages are spoken by about three-quarters (74%) of the population of the country. Indian languages merge with each other and are not separated by hard and fast boundaries. There is an intermingling of languages as well as cultures among the various linguistic groups. Nine out of every ten persons speak at least one of the eighteen scheduled languages. In most areas people are often bilingual or even tri-lingual. The bilingualism is wide spread among all classes except the peasantry of linguistically homogenous areas. This significantly large group of individuals share a common link involving language, culture, customs or geographical location as depicted in figure –3.

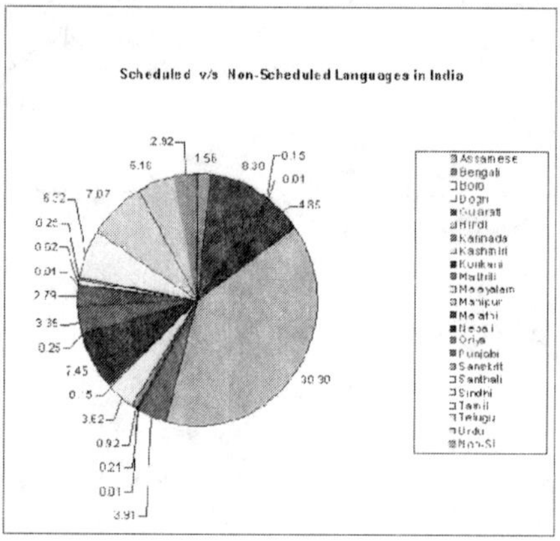

Figure 3 - (Languages Spoken in India, 2013) and Appendix 1

Current Trends in English

Sarma (2012) in his article titled 'Osum' Shakespeare and the 'mincemeat of English' which was published in India's leading newspaper' The Hindu 'states that in India "People tend to express anguish and anger at the way English is used in Facebook". Many Indians tend to call facebook the 'Facebook' since they find it invading their homes and corrupting the strictly brought up orthodox, traditional children with worldly idealisms and unacceptable western values. He claims that "English is not monolithic or monochromatic in its structures since its polyphonic nature lends itself to experimentation. During the period of Old English between 500ADto100AD, coining new words which were then called 'kennings' like Ofer hronrade hyra scolde – translated into Modern English as over whale-road" (Sarma, 2012) was prevalent.

In India, the educated elite are mostly familiar with only one form of English, which is, 'Standard English', and they are usually not familiar with other dialects, for example cockney which writers like Shaw and Eliot explored. Educated native English speakers tend not to be familiar with the dialectal variations of English, their pronunciation or syntax. The Australian nasal twang, for example, makes "day" sound like "die".: confusion abounds when an Australian visitor to India is apparently telling his "Standard English" hosts, quite cheerfully, "I have arrived to die." Consequently any deviation from 'Standard English' makes us feel that English is being 'butchered' though such variations and deviations are viewed as inevitable processes.

Even in the Old English period there were four main dialectal forms which were Mercian, Northumbrian, Kentish and West Saxon of which West Saxon slowly acquired supremacy due to the influence of the great King Alfred (Hogg & Denison, 2006). During the Middle English Period (1100 AD to 1500 AD), the dialects were Kentish, Southern, Northern, East Midland and West-Midland, of which the West-Midland seemed to have acquired greater currency. Later, several factors led to the evaluation of 'Standard English,' which gained global currency though other nonstandard dialects such as Cockney, Dorset and Scottish do exist (Hogg

However, as Trudgill (2006,p.119)states," Standard English is simply one variety of English among many and it is a sub- variety of English." One writer who is known for his extensive inventions, deviations, coinages and contractions is Shakespeare. His words came largely from a manipulation of the then current language. He coined many words by switching words from one part of speech to another. He turned nouns into verbs, adjectives into verbs, verbs into adjectives, adding prefixes and suffixes. The following is one such example of an adjective being modified as a verb.

Will all great Neptune's ocean wash this blood Clean from my hand? No, this my hand will rather the multitudinous seas incarnadine, Making the green one red (Macbeth 2-ii)

The word 'incarnadine' was used as an adjective only in Elizabethan days and Shakespeare for the first time used it as a verb.

In" The Language of Shakespeare, "Crystal(2012),refers (quoting Shakespeare) to one of his coinages thus:

Can this cockpit hold

The vasty fields of France (Henry V-prologue).

Why did Shakespeare coined a new word, 'vasty'? To have written 'the vast fields of France' would have caused an unwelcome jerkiness. (In) "The... fields of France' we need a two-beat adjective to fill the gap, expressive of great size; 'vast' is the obvious choice but it has only one syllable. Large, huge and great are available but they have wrong rhythm... adding an adjective forming suffix – y is an attractive way of solving the metrical problem"(Sarma, 2012).

Even when English was restricted to Britain during the periods Old English, Middle English and the early stages of Modern English, there were several dialectal variations. However, when English acquired an international dimension, its dialectal variations such as American English, Australian English, New Zealand English, Indian English and South African English provided a global stage for people to interact, which in fact has initiated an inevitable process for a common dialect and acceptance of various accents in the universal context. In addition this inevitable process leads to a uniform approach in social media spaces, like facebook to twitter to name a few. This can be heard frequently around as for example omitting vowels or using shortened forms such as 'osum' for 'awesome' or introducing numbersforspellings4for'for','gr8'for'great','2morrow'for tomorrow' etc. As Sarma (2012)a *professor of English* forecasts "All this might create a new dialect,' NETLINGLSH'" which only future generations can affirm as they continue the process of changing the language linguistically and phonetically with the trendy influences of modern technology.

Dialectical invention clearly leads to deviations from 'Standard English'. However a dialect is generally not treated with derision, simply because it is non-standard. This is also a sub-variety of English. If Shakespeare were to live now, he would perhaps add one more piece of work to his dramatic oeuvre by incorporating the English found on the NET.

Independent India's Choice of Language

The status and role of English in India has continued to grow consistently from colonisation through to post independence to the present day modern India of the 21'st century, where it is considered a global power house in education and economics. When India gained its independence in 1947 it had to resolve, like all previous colonies, the problem of choosing a national language for national unity, integration and identity. Being a multilingual, multicultural land, the problem was more acute for the Indian politicians. "As Per the Census of India 1951, there were 845 dialects with 15 major regional languages belonging to the four major linguistic families: Indo-Aryan, Dravidian, the Tibitan- Chinese and the Austric family of languages"(Sood,1988). When a new independent country chooses an official language it must consider more than its present national identity and unity; it must consider what will benefit the whole population during a future of increasing literacy, education and modernisation. Resolving the language question in India's multilinguistic environment proved to be a major source of controversy for more than a decade.

The language controversy was elitist in character and centred around the choice for English or Hindi. The main participants involved in the debate were the 'pro Hindi' contingent, predominantly from the Hindi-speaking Northern states like Uttar Pradesh, Madhya Pradesh, Bihar, etc. and the opposing "anti- Hindi" party from the south, confined mainly to the state of Tamil Nadu. The latter's main demand had been for the retention of English as the sole official language of the union of India, with demonstrators using slogans such as "Hindi never, English ever" (Dasgupta, 1970, p. 136). The constitution ultimately specified that Hindi, spoken in many dialects by 40 percent of Indians, would become the official language in 1965. After the transition phase through which English was spoken by the educated elite of the country and the other non-Hindi speakers, especially in the South Indian states of Tamil Nadu, Karnataka, Andhra Pradesh and Kerala mobilized political support and activism against the central government's efforts to impose Hindi. To settle the dispute, the government allowed continued use of English for states that wished to keep it. No one common language is spoken on the Indian subcontinent. Hindi and English are the co-official national languages of India, and both tongues are used as lingua francas in the various linguistic regions. In addition, the Indian constitution recognizes 18 state languages, which are used in schools and in official transactions. These are Assamese, Bengali, Gujarati, Hindi, Kannada, Kashmiri, Konkani, Malayalam, Meitheli Manipuri, Marathi, Nepali, Oriya, Punjabi, Sindhi, Tamil, Telugu, and Urdu. In Pakistan, the official language is Urdu; the official language of Bangladesh is Bengali, (India.gov. 2010).

Post-Colonial Education Metamorphosis

The status and role of English in India has evolved considerably because, the context and importance of English teaching together with the influence of the learner and the classroom teacher has drastically changed in the post- independence era. Students are exposed now, in the post- independence era to a varied levels of English in India, depending on the kind of school they attend. The schools in India can be divided into two types.

1. English-medium schools–

Mostly run by private individual businesses, social or religious organisations.

2. Regional medium schools-

Mostly public - run by the state or central governments.

Between these two extremes of education, students are exposed to different levels of English and are taught very differently. Broadly they can be tabulated as below.

Table–A English Language Education in Schools in India

Type of school	*Medium of Instructions*	*Introduction of English as a subject*	*Total value of exposure*
Private	E	Pre Primary 3+	15 years
Government	R		
Central/ model aided	Language English	Grade 1- 6+	12 years
State government run	Regional Language	Grade 1- 6+	10-12 years
Central government run	Regionale Language	Grade 6- 12+	2-7 years

Source: (Sood ,1988)

Moreover, because of such tactically introduced political policies impact on its initial education programs India is now recognized globally for its vast talent pool of English-speaking, well-educated professionals (Khokhar, 2006). From being a language rooted in colonialism, English has become the language that has given India an edge over countries where English is a foreign language. India has become are source pool of English, a language who se ascendancy remains unquestioned. English plays an important role in the domains of education, administration, business and political relations, judiciary, industry, and is therefore a passport to social mobility, higher education, and better job opportunities. Indeed, in urban India, it is very common to see young people codemixing and code-switching between English and other Indian languages.

Further more, English literature written by Indian authors has made its mark in world literature. Rabindranath Tagore was the first to get Nobel prize for literature. Among the Indian writers in English, R. K. Narayan chooses to write in English because he himself says ,"It is the only language I am really familiar with. It is the only language which is transparent and takes on the hues of the country or region where the story is set" (Narayan, 2006). The flexibility and adaptability of English has fascinated him, and for this reason he has chosen it as his medium of story-telling.

Once independence was gained and the English ended their colonial rule, the perception of English as having an alien power- base changed; however, controversy about the role of English has continued to this day(Crystal,2008). Kachru notes that "English now has national and international functions that are both distinct and complementary. English has thus acquired a new power-base and a new elitism", (2001). While only about three percent of India's population speaks English as a first-language, they are the individuals who lead India's economic, industrial, professional, political, and social life. Even though English is primarily a second-language for many more, it is the medium in which a great number of the interactions in the above domains are carried out.

Currently English is the written and spoken language of commerce, finance and business, and the language that most brings together people from different cultures, nations, ethnicity and languages electronically through the World Wide Web and education in every sphere of life around the world. Enormous amount of information can be accessed through the internet as long as one is familiar with English. British Council data shows that the English language is the main discourse of books, newspapers, airports and air-traffic control, international business and academic conferences, science, technology, diplomacy, sport, international competitions, pop music and advertising. Over two- thirds of the world's scientists read in English and three quarters of the world's mail is written in English (British Council, 2008). Eighty percent of the world's electronically stored information is in English and of the estimated 200 million users of the Internet, some thirty-six percent communicate in English.(Crystal,2008). As for the spoken word, although estimates of how many people speak a language can never be completely precise and therefore vary considerably, English is considered the second most widely- spoken language in the world after Mandarin.

The growth of English as a spoken language had its origins in the 16th century when between 1558 and 1603, English speakers in the world are thought to have numbered between 5 and 7 million, (Crystal, 2008). Four hundred years later, the number of English speakers has increased almost fifty fold with Randolph Quirk estimating in *The Use of English* (1968) that by 1962,250 million would have been using English as a mother-tongue, while a further 100 million would have been using it as a second or foreign language (Quirk, 1968). Joshua Fishman and his colleagues, in '*The Spread of English*', go even further, calculating that as many as 300 million use English as their mother tongue. Bailey and Gorlach in their book '*English as a World Language*' in 1982 have also quoted these figures (Bailey & Görlach, 1983; Fishman, 1987). By 1984 English mother-tongue use was said to be 300 million with secondlanguage use also at 300 million, and foreign language-use at 100 million, (Crystal, 2008). What this means is that English is currently one of the most widely spoken and written languages worldwide, with some 375 million native speakers and over 750 million people speaking English as a foreign language, (Crystal, 2008). Of the 163 member nations of the U.N., more use English as their official language than any other. English has official or special status in at least seventy five countries with a total population of over two billion and one out of four of the world's population speak English to some level of competence with over one billion people learning English currently, (Crystal, 2008). A simple measure used to calculate the economic influence of a language is to add up the gross domestic products (GDP) of all the nations where it is spoken. People who count English as their mother-tongue make up less than 10% of the world's population, but possess over 30% of the world's economic power (Coleman, 2011).

It is the figure for English as an "official language", estimated at over 1,400 million (Sarwal, 2004), that keeps dramatically growing. For example, presently more than a third of the population of India alone is capable of carrying on a domestic conversation in English. '*India Today*' a leading monthly publication's survey in 1997 confirms this figure, reaching the same conclusion (Kachru, 2001). Given that India's population is now well over a billion, this means a total of around 350 million people speak English well, which is more than the combined English- speaking populations of all the leading first-language countries.

The 'Demographic Divide' and the Necessity for Education in English

In the year 2004 India had a population of 1,080 million, of whom 672 million people were in the age-group 15 to 64 years. This is usually treated as the "working age population". Since outside of this age group very few people work, it is reasonable to think of the remainder, that is, 408 million people, as the "dependent population". A nation's "dependency ratio" is the ratio of the dependent population to the working-age population. In the case of India this turns out to be 0.6. On this score India does not look too different from many other developing countries. Bangladesh's dependency ratio is 0.7, Pakistan's 0.8, Brazil's 0.5. (Bloom, Canning et al. 2007). What is different about India is the prediction that it will see a sharp decline in its dependency ratio over the next 30 years or so. This is what constitutes the demographic dividend for India. India's fertility rate - that is, the average number of children a woman expects to have in her life time - used to be 3.8 in 1990. (Basu, 2007). This has fallen to 2.9 and is expected to fall further. Since women had higher fertility earlier, India now has a sizeable number of people in the age group 0-15 years. Nonetheless since fertility is falling, some 10 or 15 years down the road, this swell of young people would have moved into the working-age category. Besides, at that time, the relative number of children will be small, thanks to the lowered fertility; India's dependency ratio would be lower. It is expected that, in 2020, the average age of an Indian will be 29 years, compared to 37 for China and 48 for Japan; and, by 2030, India's dependency ratio should be just over

This can confer many benefits. First, there is the direct benefit of a rise in the relative number of bread-winners. Moreover, with fewer children being born, more women are expected to join the work force, giving a further fillip to the bread-winner ratio. A more indirect but vital benefit for the economy is the effect this will have on savings. Since people save most during the working years of their lives as when they are children, they clearly consume more than they earn, and the situation is the same during old age, a decline in the nation's dependency ratio should be associated with a rise in the average savings rate. The significance of these figures becomes clearer when we compare them with what they were just a few decades ago. In 1939 the average Life Expectancy of an Indian was 23 years with 6,000,000 annual deaths of which 44% were due to malaria. In some provinces like Bengal: 750,000 under the age of 15 years died each year (Stanley, 1939).

India's savings rate as a percentage of GDP has been rising since 2003. It now stands at 33% which is comparable to the Asian superperformers, all of whom save at above 30%, with China saving at an astonishing near 40% rate. This savings growth is driven by improvements in the government's fiscal health and a sharp rise in corporate savings. But even if these factors disappear, the decline in the dependency ratio should enable India to hold its savings and investment rate above the 30% mark for the next 25 years.

This theory of demographic advantage has been challenged by some as just that - theory. One way of evaluating this in reality is to look at the actual experience of other nations. The most striking example of economic growth being spurred by demography is the case of Ireland. Ireland's legalisation of contraception in 1979 caused a decline in the birth rate, from 22 (per 1000 population) in 1980 to 13 in 1994 (Basu, 2007). This caused a rapid decline in the dependency ratio. The phenomenal economic boom in Ireland thereafter, earning it the sobriquet "Celtic Tiger", is very likely founded in this fertility decline. One has seen a similar sequence of changes in demographics and the economy in Japan in the 1950s and China in the 1980s. The expectation is that India will get benefit in terms of higher savings and investment rates and this will continue to fire India's high growth rate.

Beyond these demographic factors, much of India's economic future will depend on how the nation performs on primary and secondary education. To make sure that the larger working-age population conferred by the demographic dividend are well educated and that the manufacturing sector which is needed to create job opportunities for the larger labour force is viable, skilled and articulate with the knowledge of English language is vital for the progress of India as a nation.

English came to India with the commercial opportunities brought forth by the British merchants as the prevalence of English as a common language in India is a legacy of the British who colonized the country and the world at large. The root of English in the Indian Subcontinent can be traced back to the incident of 31st December, 1600, when Queen

Elizabeth I granted a charter to a few merchants of London, giving them a monopoly of trade with India. Confronted with a new, exotic, and diverse culture, the British rulers struggled to articulate their experience in India and to communicate effectively with the natives. Their subjects found themselves equally at a loss to communicate with them (Warsi, 2008).

The slow expansion and colonisation of the Subcontinent meant that English language and culture progressed at a slow pace into orthodox Indian society in the early 1600's, when the East India Company started trading and English missionaries first began their efforts at conversion. Simultaneously, a large number of Christian schools imparting an English language education were set up by the early 1800's. The process of producing English proficient bilinguals in India began with the colonial government's "Minute of 1835", which officially endorsed the Supreme Council of India member T.B. Macaulay's goal of forming "a class who may be interpreters between us and the millions whom we govern a class of persons, Indians in blood and colour, but English in taste, in opinion, in morals and in intellect" (Macaulay, 1835, pp. 107-117). It is generally supposed by modern historians that the study of English was imposed upon Indians by Lord Macaulay from the Supreme Council of India who was heavily involved in redrafting the Indian penal code and the promotion of education in India with the sole purpose of serving the colonial ends of maintaining the British administration in and control of India. The British Raj's 'Anglicization of Indian Education' was established between the period 1765 and 1947 with British patronage and encouragement for the English Language with the establishment of three universities at Bombay currently known us Mumbai, and Calcutta, which is today's Kolkatta, and Madras, currently called Chennai. By 1928 English in India had become the language of the elite, of the administration and the media, though the press claimed only a limited circulation, while Indian literature in English was developing at a rapid rate (Kachru, 1983). Accordingly English permeated some of the most important parts of society: the government and civil service, the media, the education system, the legal system, and gradually the social sphere as well. Today, India is recognized globally for its vast talent pool of English speaking, well-educated professionals because of these tactically introduced policies (Khokhar, 2006). Now, as then, English is a means by which India secures its economic future.

Linguistics is a study of the systems and principles underlying human languages. Language is an arbitary system of articulated sounds made use of by human beings for communication and expression. It is useful to set up different but inter-related levels of analysis to describe the sounds, words, sentences and meanings of human languages,

Linguists have set up phonological, morphological, lexical, syntactic and semantic levels of analysis (Verma & Krishnamoorthy, 1989) where Phonology is the study of the organisation of the units of the sounds of speech into syllables and other larger units. Phonetics is the study of the articulation, transmission and reception of a description of the systems and patters of sounds that occur in that language (Verma & Krishnaswamy, 1989).

Distinguishing Characteristics of Indian English

There is a general assumption that Indian English is very similar to British English , but this assumption is mostly based on superficial observations of lexical similarities. It is to be observed that not every linguistic item is used by the Indian English-speaker and that a great deal of regional and educational differentiation exists. One can find a number of distinctive characteristics at phonological, morphological, lexical and syntactic levels. "India has had a longer exposure to English than any other country that uses it as a second-language, and its distinctive words, idioms, grammar, rhetoric and rhythms are numerous and pervasive" (Crystal, 2004, p. 1). The English language spread throughout the colonies of the British Empire during the period of its expansion in the 18th and 19th centuries. As a result, the lingua franca of India today is English, perceived by adults and teens alike as socially and professionally indispensable. As Smith (1997) confirms, the prestige value of the language remains one of primary reasons for using English in India. Communication in English is fashionable and considered progressive in virtually every field: teenagers pick out English expressions from the music they listen to; businessmen feel a need to demonstrate their mastery of commercial English; TV and newspaper journalists want to make it clear that they are not lagging behind (Smith, 1997).

Distinctions in Phonology, Morphology and Lexicon

Moreover phonetics involves the study of the physical aspect of sounds through production and the perception of sounds, called phones. However, Phonology is about the abstract aspect of sounds and it studies the phonemes which are those sounds that can bring a difference in meaning between two words. Trudgill & Hannah (1994) claim that the English alveolar /t/ would be articulated as the Indian retroflex /t/ or as the dental /t/ in different phonological environments. The result was that the retroflex completely replaced the alveolar; in fact, it has been found that the entire series of English alveolar consonants tends to be replaced by retroflex consonants (Trudgill & Hannah, 1994).

Indian English speakers have a tendency to drop the – ed ending after /k/ and /t/ (eg. walked became walk, visited became visit). The articulation of / t / as in then), which normally is pronounced as interdental /d/, but which sometimes seemed to become alveoloar. Sometimes a was used in front of vowel initial words before which American English and British English speakers would use an. This is a very natural adjustment for native speakers, yet it seems to require conscious effort for some Indian English speakers (Baldridge, 2002). Indian English tends to have a reduced vowel system, /r/ tends to become a flap or retroflex flap; the consonants /p/, /t/ and /k/ tend to be unaspirated, and in some regions /v/ and /w/ are not distinguished ("volley ball" emerges as "wally ball"). Indian English tends to be syllable rather than stress-timed. Also, syllables that would be unstressed in other varieties of English receive some stress in Indian English and thus do not have reduced vowels. Suffixes tend to be stressed, and function words which are weak in other varieties of English (of, to, etc.) tend not to be reduced in Indian English (Trudgill & Hannah, 1994).

Thiruvalluvar, one of the greatest Tamil poets of the 100 BC has written in his 648th Kural, "Words used in their proper order and in a pleasing manner would readily be accepted and obliged by the world" (Nayak, 2002), highlighting the importance of effective communication (Kanthimathi, 2007). Under the influence of the mother tongue Indian English produces compounds, such as cousin-brother, cousin-sister, paternal-aunt, maternal-aunt, and this particular function is inherent in the terminology of Indian languages. Other compounds include chalkpiece, key-bunch, pindrop silence, railway station, bus stand, etc. Sometimes compound words are used to give different connotations, 'tea garden' in Indian English means tea estate / plantation, whereas in British English it means a garden in which tea or other refreshments are served to the public. A number of words from Indian languages are assimilated in English, namely, aaya (Tamil) = house maid, kuuli (Tamil) = labourer. Indians also pluralize many English mass nouns, and end with words such as litters, furnitures, woods, roties (bread) etc. Sometimes words which should be pluralized are not, for instance, one of my relative, one of the student.

Words such as time-pass, chumma (Tamil) 'without any purpose' have also crept into Indian English. Indian English has shortened forms of many words, for example, princi = principal, lab asst = laboratory assistant, enthu = enthusiasm. One also comes across distinctive usages, such as pre-owned cars (used cars), near and dear ones (friends and relatives), and kitchen platform (work- surface). In the matrimonial columns, we find interesting coinages, such as weatish = brown, professionally qualified = educated. These are all indicators of linguistic reflection and social change. English words are sometimes pronounced differently by Indians because they are following their mother-tongue pattern. Vowels which have been dropped by American and British English speakers are typically articulated by Indians. For example, 'typically' is generally pronounced ti-pick-lee, but Indian English speakers will often say ti-pick-ah-lee.

Many new words and usages appear in Indian English. A food grinder (small) is simply called a 'mixi'. A bigger grinder that is used to grind rice and other grains for idly or dosai is called a 'wet grinder'. A person who is modern and fashionable is termed 'fast'. A 'deadly' movie or event is hard-hitting and action packed, while 'hi-tech outfit' and 'hitech movie' are common usages. For an Indian doing mathematics, two into four means 2x4 and two by four is 2/4 or two divided by four.

Distinctions in Syntax

Syntax deals with the combination of words into phrases, clauses and sentences at the syntactic level, the uses of the articles a and the are arbitrary in Indian English, one is substituted for a as in 'one beautiful girl' instead of 'a beautiful girl'. The and a are often dropped when they should be used, and used when they should be left out, as in, for example, 'They are going to school'. Another interesting discovery is the use of only and itself to emphasize time and place, e.g., 'she is coming now only' and 'can I get tomorrow itself'. To emphasize an action, Indian English speakers often use reduplication. For example 'good, good', 'run, run' fast, fast; long, long hair, etc. The word 'take' is used to mean 'consume' any food items: Will you take tea or coffee? The word 'keep' is used instead of 'put', as in, 'keep the ball there'; 'put' is often used without an explicit destination or direction, as in, 'shall I put the tape?' One of the most characteristic traits of Indian English grammar is the use of the progressive aspect with habitual actions, completed actions, and stative verbs. This produces sentences such as "I am doing it often" rather than "I do it often", "where are you coming from?" instead of "where have you come from?" and "she was having many sarees" rather than "she had many sarees", (Trudgill & Hannah, 1994). A number of other syntactic variations are found in Indian English, such as,

Where you go?	=	Where do you go?
Where you are going?	=	Where are you going?
Did you studied well?	=	Did you study well?
He/she do not know that	=	He/she does not know that

As can be seen here, the word-order of questions, in particular, is often reworked in Indian English.

It is claimed that Indian English is nearer to British English than to American English. Indians cite many examples of words they use in common with British English. They fail to realize that on a deeper linguistic level, Indian English differs from British English just as much as from American

English. They are mutually distinct varieties and that uniqueness should be valued and appreciated.

India has incorporated English into a working language that has its own linguistic and cultural ecologies and socio-cultural contexts (Baldridge, 2002). However there is a 'clash' between the system of the first-language and that of the second. When one language system becomes more or less a habit, the learning of a second-language, in this case English, becomes rather difficult.

The mistakes made in the second-languages are often due to:

1. the "gravitational pull" of the first-language / mother tongue
2. Internal analogy and over-generalization, e.g. Childrens, furnitures, teached, bringed, a milk, etc.
3. Pronunciation according to spelling.
4. exposure to a non-standard variety
5. failure to understand the nature of the second-language
6. the cultural gap between the two systems.

Second-language learners commit errors; 'mistakes' that get fossilized are errors. A learner's so-called errors are systematic and it is precisely this regularity which shows that the learner is following a set of rules. These rules are not those of the target language but a 'transitional' form of language similar in many respect to the target language, but also similar to the learner's mother tongue, or indeed any other language the learner may already command (Verma & Krishnaswamy, 1989).

In the meantime, the Indian presence in Britain marks the other end of the linguistic continuity. Following several generations of immigration (Crystal, 2004), British people have become familiar with the British dialects of Indian English and it can been declared that Indians have made English into a native language and claimed Indian English as its very own. Its distinctive functions has etched English into the everyday life of India and its citizens, and it has become a part of being an Indian, though the language expertise might not be easily comprehensible. Countless Indians feel that the use of English should be actively encouraged because of the limitless opportunities it confers into the global academic, intellectual and scientific arena (Baldridge, 2002).

Language change happens within the limits of human languages because of their built-in tendency to change, the inventive faculty of the users, several other human factors like modesty, confusion, slot and the passage of time.

1. When the users of a language get tired of saying the same thing in the same way they want to escape from the humdrum.Sometimes we 'telephone' sometimes we 'phone', at times we 'ring up' and occasionally we 'call up' or 'call'.
2. New realities may force the users of a language to invent or coin new words or phrases. 'Brunch' is a combination of 'breakfast' and 'lunch', 'motel' is derived from 'motorist's hotel'.
3. The tendency to abridge, which may be a result of sloth, produces shorter, units ('mike' for 'microphone', 'telly' for 'television', 'doc' for 'doctor' etc.) and the shortened form becomes popular.
4. It is found that, what is used in a dialect today may become part of a standard language tomorrow A language may change as the result of contact with other languages. (Verma and Krishnaswamy, 1989).

Chapter - 3

English as a Global Language

A Common World Language

Communications have been greatly improved by the widespread adoption of mass media especially radio and television coupled with reduced costs and time that has been made possible by the use of new technologies, such as satellites, computers and mobile telephones. The Internet is quickly emerging as the preferred information highway to meet our daily communication needs as well as for conducting important business transactions.

It is now almost impossible for people to fully participate in the global village that they live in without 'knowing' a common world language. In fact, new linguistic insights have shown that no human language is superior to any other and that the development and growth of a language depend upon its use (Sarwal, 2011). Moreover languages cannot have any independent existence since it solely exists in the brain, mouth, ears, hands and eyes of the user, than on any mystical space or even literary form. Meanwhile, English, for various reasons primarily due to British rule in the many parts of the world has emerged as the popular lingua franca. In the process, it must be acknowledged, the role of English and its functions have vastly changed. English is no longer seen as the language of rulers, or as an instrument for promoting British culture and values. Tom McArthur, (2003), the famous linguist in his introduction to *The Oxford Companion to the English Language* claims that it has been towards the very end of the twentieth century that the

English language has become a global resource. Hence it cannot be claimed that it does not owe its very existence, patronage or the defense of its very nature and uniqueness to any nation or group.

It cannot be forgotten that according to the English Language Guide (2013), English is currently used in over 70 countries as an official or semiofficial language, and plays a very significant role in 20 others. Over 1,400 million people live in countries where there is a tradition of using English. Some 75% of the world's mail and world's information is stored in English. Of the estimated 50 million users of the Internet, a majority use English McArthurr,(2003). With the evolution of English to the status of a world language (or 'English as a 'global' language') some of the necessary features of a world language have emerged. Irrespective of its origin, a world language must become a utility language that embraces the needs of everyone and be accepted by many countries around the world. Though English originally was the language of the British, the many varieties of English, now include American English, African English, Indian English and Australian English. Moreover, English is now the medium for the dreams and aspirations of many people and experiences of diverse nations. It is used to transmit a mass of various information, whether it be the latest advances in the fields of science and technology, the experiences of an ethnic group, negotiations in the field of commerce, documentation of cultural ethos or individual experiences. Its vocabulary has been vastly enriched with the inclusion of many new words from other languages of the world. Some ten thousand words derived from Hindi and other Indian languages have become a part of Indian English, (Crystal, 2003).

In general what marks out a global language is not that it is commonly spoken, merely, or that it is superior in its vocabulary or syntax, or that it is easy to learn, but that it happens to be at a particular time a language has power and influence. Latin was a world language during the Roman conquests whose influence declined with the decline of Roman military power. It was not the grammatical easiness, size of its vocabulary, intrinsic structural properties, logical beauty and simplicity of this language that made it popular since Latin was the language of the elite for generations, in spite of its difficult inflections, as was Greek, Arabic and ancient Sanskrit. To illustrate the point, History has given us Greek, the language of communication in the Middle East two thousand years ago. It was not the intellects of Plato and Aristotle but the forceful military might of Alexander the Great 's army that made the language of his people "global", as was the case also with the Legions of the Roman Empire spreading Latin and the Islamic wars spreading Arabic. As David Crystal puts it, "A language has traditionally become an international language for one chief reason: the power of its people especially their political and military power" (Crystal 2003).

Power cannot be maintained without money and this factor played a crucial role in the English language's evolution into today's global language. "It may take a militarily powerful nation to establish a language but it takes an economically powerful one to maintain and expand it" (Crystal, 2003). Britain's position as the world's leading industrial and trading country at a crucial period in the early nineteenth century, dominating the political arena of the world, and the gradual appearance into the world forum of the United States of America as an independent but fast growing economic country subsequently helped the establishment of English as the language of communication, politics, media, technology and education. The emergence of large multinational organisations that were growing at an unprecedented pace with the help of technological advancements in communications and the ever expanding world of trade fostered by the commercial media, opened the avenue for the total dominance of English as a global '*lingua franca', or 'common language'* in the twentieth century. Crystal advocates to the theory that "British political imperialism had sent English around the globe, during the nineteenth century, so that it was a language 'on which the sun never sets'. During the twentieth century, this world presence was maintained and promoted almost single-handedly through the economic supremacy of the new American superpower. Economics replaced politics as the chief driving force. And the language behind the dollar was English." (2003, p10). The status of a '*lingua franca', or 'common language'* has through the centuries been governed by the political might and dominance of the people speaking it, as Latin by the Roman conquerors and Greek by Alexander the Great and other Greek philosophers. In today's world regional languages like Arabic in the Middle East, Swahali in South Africa and Hindi in the Asian sub-continent have developed into minor '*lingua franca*', in their respective limited areas of dominance.

In the present day international scenario a crucial issue faced by most planning committees is the sensitive issue of the choice of main language, however participants are as a utilitarian measure automatically using English as a 'working language', because predominantly it is the most common language that they for some reason or the other have learnt and are competent in as members of a very fast-paced global community. There is now a widespread consensus among major international organisations and collaborations that it is more practical and viable to try to reduce the number of languages involved in world bodies to make it possible to cut down on the massive amount of interpretation/ translation and clerical work Half the budget of an international organization can easily get swallowed up in translation costs. But trimming a translation budget is never easy, as obviously no country likes the thought of its language being given a reduced international standing. The need for a global language is particularly appreciated by the international academic and business communities, and it is here that the adoption of a single lingua franca is most in evidence, both in lecturerooms and board-rooms, as well as in thousands of individual contacts being made daily all over the globe (Crystal, 2003, p. 12).

Individuals in the shrinking global environment have become more mobile, both physically and electronically towards communication with fingertip access to telephones through mobiles and to data or information through the internet. Personal physical appearance and other material forms of evidence are no longer required for the negotiating and signing of multimillion dollar contracts as business has, in effect, dissolved country and continental borders to create a 'Global Village' where information is sent and received electronically, simultaneously to any one and to any number of individuals. The whole face of the modern world is changing on a day to day basic with the rapid strides in technological advancement.

History has no precedent for the dramatic changes happening in the present day world; never before have so many nations been engaged in productive dialogue for a better world, nor have so many people travelled for business and pleasure across national and language borders. A tremendous amount of tension is being placed on translation and interpreting and the widespread move towards bilingualism is growing greatly to ease the burden on professionals and for the establishment of a global language. (Crystal, 2003) But, David Crystal suggests, there is another possible eventuality.

Crystal (2003, p. 12) points out that a global language could "cultivate an elite monolingual linguistic class" who could be complacent and dismissive in their attitude towards other languages, with those having it as their mother-tongue tending to use their familiarity with the language to their advantage. Their achieving of dominance by thinking and working quickly in their mother-tongue at the expense of others would have the effect of creating a linguistic chasm between the rich and the poor. The opportunity and necessity to learn other languages would also dissolve with the establishment of a global language, sounding the death knell for minority languages with chauvinists celebrating one language's triumphant success over the other (Graddol, 2006). Mankind cannot return to the innocence of the days prior to the 'Tower of Babel', before the birth of multilingualism; the fact that the use of a single language by a community does not assure peace and harmony as has been proven over and over again in world history, as in the American Civil War, Spanish Civil War, Vietnam War, and in Ireland, Yugoslavia, Korea etc.. On the other hand, multilingual coexistence has been proving to be very sustainable and possible in various parts of the world, as can be seen in Switzerland, Finland, India, Singapore and perhaps most of all in the U.S. which could be the globe's most language-diverse multicultural and cosmopolitan country comparable to what Australia or Canada are aiming towards.

An individual's lack of knowledge of English obviously does not of itself retard his intellectual ability, but lack of English may impair his ability to make his knowledge available and prevent its being acknowledged. Very considerable advantages emerge when a global language is promoted through effective childhood education. Human beings are born with capabilities and abilities for bilingualism and these should not be permitted to fall into disuse. "There are clear signs of growing awareness, within English-speaking communities, of the need to break away from the traditional monolingual bias" (Crystal, 2003, p.18).

Concept of English as a Lingua Franca and its Development

In the discussion of English as a second-language as early as the 1980s, Kachru (1985) elaborates on the status of English in a number of different communities in the world. Speakers of English are categorised into three groups in which English is used as a first-language (L1), as a second-language (L2) and as a foreign language (FL). Kachru identifies these groups as the 'Inner Circle' countries, the 'Outer Circle' countries and the 'Expanding Circle' countries respectively. Based on this way of showing the world status of English, Seidlhofer, (2004) presents an extensive review of recent work on English as a lingua franca. English, as viewed by her, though labeled variably by different authors as 'English as an international language', 'a lingua franca', 'a global language' or 'a world language', is used internationally not only by the Expanding Circle people but also by speakers of English as a native language in all its dialects (i.e. Kachru's Inner Circle) and speakers of New Englishes (i.e. Kachru 's Outer Circle) (Seidlhofer, 2004).

The term *lingua franca* was originally used to denote an intermediary language used by speakers of Arabic with travellers from Western Europe (House, 2003). Its meaning was then extended to refer to a language of commerce. Such a meaning is clearly not sufficient in describing today's global English. Instead, several definitions have been provided to define a lingua franca from a formal perspective. Samarin, for example, characterises the term as "any lingua medium of communication between people of different mother tongues, for whom it is a second- language"(Samarin, 1987 cited in Seidlhofer, 2004, p. 211). The notion that lingua franca interactions involve no native speakers is also adopted in other definitions, which specify that ELF is a "contact language between persons who share neither a common native tongue nor a common culture" (Firth, 1996, p. 240) and that "ELF interactions are defined as interactions between members of two or more different lingua cultures in English, for none of whom English is the mother tongue" (House, 1999, p.74).

While these definitions portray EIL in its original, simplest form, referring exclusively to English use between speakers whose mother-tongue is not English, recent literature has highlighted ELF communication in the global use, avoiding a narrow view of the language (Knapp & Meierkord, 2002; Seidlhofer, 2001, 2004). Seidlhofer (2004) emphasises that the current use of ELF is also associated with speakers from the Inner and Outer Circles and ELF interactions indeed have taken place in these contexts, simultaneously involving speakers of English from all three Circles. She perceives that such interactions are increasing now and the trend is likely to continue in the future partly because these interactions often occur in certain significant fields such as international business, politics, science, technology and media discourse, which are indeed the result of global development in these fields. In these interactions, English plays the role of a useful tool for communication that cannot be conducted in the L1 languages, and ELF speakers are not concerned with achieving or approaching the standard norms of English native speakers. Instead, their main concerns are usually focused primarily on maintaining efficiency, relevance, and economy in the language learning process and in the language use (Seidlhofer, 2001). While members of different L1 communities have much more occasion to talk in English both among themselves and with native English speakers in such ELF interactions, there is a question concerning whether the English they use has changed over time. To further her discussion, Seidlhofer refers to House's ideas, noting:

It seems vital to pay more attention to the nature of ELF interactions, and ask whether and how they are different from both interactions between native speakers and non-native speakers. An answer to this question would bring us closer to finding out whether and in what ways ELF interactions are actually sui generic (House, 1999,

As House (2003) asserts, it is crucial to reconsider the current contexts in which ELF operates and identifying possible reasons for the spread of the language. Seidlhofer (2004) describes the current global linguistic situation in the following terms, suggesting one important aspect behind the development.

For the first time in history, a language has reached truly global dimensions, and as a consequence, is being shaped, in its international uses, at least as much by its non-native speakers as its native speakers. This process has been accelerated by the dramatic expansion of electronic communication through the internet (Seidlhofer, 2004, p. 211).

Another factor considered by Seidlhofer (2004) to contribute to language development involves the changes in English-speaking environments. The language is now used more and more for practical purposes by many people who possess varied norms and levels of proficiency. This has led to a remarkable feature of the environment in which English is used, namely that the number of non-native speakers is substantially larger than that of native speakers. The relationship is confirmed by Graddol (1997) to be about four to one. This also means that an increasingly large number of interactions in English occur between participants whose standards of grammar, lexis and pronunciation do not conform to any recognised norms. This point is consonant with Melchers and Shaw (2003, p. 195) observation that there is a process of internalisation and destandardisation where "nonstandard, unedited English is becoming more visible".

Out of these arguments a conclusion is made about ELF that the language "has taken on a life of its own, independent to a considerable degree of the norms established by its native users, and that warrants recognition" (Seidlhofer, 2004, p. 212). As Seidlhofer (2004) explains, ELF will become the preferred term pertinent to English for worldwide communication not because lingua franca definitions theoretically confine ELF interactions within non-native user communication as discussed above but because the term can best illustrate the trend that it is these non- native users who provide the strongest motivation for the spread and development of the language.

English language pedagogy also has implications on the development of ELF. It is clear that the active agents of the transmission of English worldwide are actually teachers of English in EFL contexts. In English language courses, even a textbook with its Inner Circle "authenticity" cannot meet the wide range of social and functional needs of all educational contexts since simulated communicative situations mentioned in textbooks do not cover all real-life interactions. Moreover, native authorities are often not available to handle every question or issue that may arise in language classrooms. Thus, non-native language teachers are the ones that "give both shape and substance to the language they spread", based on their own judgment and creativity. And while these non-native teachers may unconsciously contribute to language change, they also play an active role in the development of the world language, as "agents of language change" (Brutt- Griffler, 1998, p. 387).

Is English the Lingua Franca

English language is increasingly being used in the "Expanding circle" (Jenkins, 2009) where people do not speak English as a first or second-language but as a foreign language to serve their needs. Therefore, ELF can be defined as a common language among non-native speakers who do not share the same language or cultural backgrounds and for whom English is not their mother-tongue (Jenkins, 2009; Kirkpatrick, 2010). Communication and mutual understanding among non-native English speakers is the tent of ELF. The base of ELF is to communicate successfully among people with different lingua background without trying to mimic native speakers proficiency (Kirkpatrick, 2010) and, as Bamgbose claimed, "it is people, not language codes, that understand one another" (Bambgbose, 1998, as cited in Seidlhofer, 2009). Scholars of ELF strongly believe that language means communication and naturally it goes under a process of changes and developments (Cogo & Jenkins, 2010).

The concept of ELF helps non-native speakers from the 'Expanding Circle' to use the language unrestrictedly and to be free from native speakers' reservations. It also supports the idea that the English use of non-native speakers should no longer be compared with that of native speakers but in terms of their own ability to English skilfully and successfully since the existence merely of variations of accent and usage doesn't reflect on competence, (Cogo & Jenkins, 2010). English speakers of all varieties should be respected according to their ability to communicate well with each other.

The ultimate purpose of ELF speakers is to communicate with each other successfully. Jenkins disputes that being able to communicate with other different mother-language speakers effectively is of greater importance than achieving English native speakers competence and Seidlhofer also seems to believe that reaching mutual understanding in communication is the main target (Jenkins, 2009; Seidlhofer, 2006, as cited in Park & Wee, 2011). On the other hand, Canagarajah (2006) argues that being a "multidialectal" is essential. On this view, speakers from all three circles – 'Inner' which is from the native speaker countries, 'Outer' who would be those who speak English as a second- language and the 'Expanding' - should have the skill to interact with each other successfully. However this would require a global proficiency in English quite inconceivable. Now that English has become the common language of the majority of people in the world it is illogical to expect that there shall ever be one model for all.

English is greatly used for practical purposes including business. Several studies have proved that English is widely and increasingly used among business workers and it might maintain its high status among other languages for the next fifty years (Kankaanranta & Louhiala- Salminen, 2007). For instance, Kankaanranta (2006) found that in spite the fact that Swedish is the second official language in Finland, the use of English has accelerated between Finnish-Swedish business, particularly in the internal communication among the employees. English has become so important in France that, although France has banned the use of languages other than French in official documents (unless they cannot find a French synonym, in which case translation into French is required), advertising agencies don't scruple to use English in their advertisements. 53% of French magazine advertisements and 80% of the brand names come from English terms (Ruellot, 2011). The number of business terms that have been borrowed from English have risen from 13.3% in 1999 to 17.5% in 2007 (Ruellot, 2011). It can be clearly seen that English has a great function in France and other expanding circle countries and the reason for this needs to be understood. Ruellot (2011) claims that English appears in French advertising because it is associated with high quality, prestige and safety; that positive attitudes towards business and technological products are being identified with English language. In this respect English as a lingua franca plays a significant role in global business communication as English is mainly used to attract international and national costumers (Ruellot, 2011).

Numerous business workers use English language as a means of communication in their work. Around 80% or more of English business practitioners are non-native speakers (Kankaanranta & Louhiala- Salminen, 2007). This shows that ELF is highly accepted among a large number of business and technology workers (Jenkins, 2009) and it also shows why there is no need to obtain a native speaker level of competence in order to achieve international business communication (Kankaanranta & Louhiala-Salminen, 2007) since English has exercised a similarly pervasive influence on the technology system.

Modern technology has imposed a new style of communication upon communities internationally. Numerous technology developments in most aspects of life, such as the internet, trade, travel and media have shaped new relationships between countries. The languages and cultures of such countries have changed in a way that reflects their new social and economic relationships (Canagarajah, 2006). The development of electronic technology has brought numerous changes in ways of communication and therefore ELF is the form of language that is expected to be able to absorb the great adjustment required by these emergent changes (Seidlhofer, 2009). Martin (2008, as cited in Ruellot, 2011) observed that the adoption of English terms in the field of information technology had accelerated. For example, high tech, application services and infrastructure services are common words which come from English (Ruellot, 2011). As Phillipson (2001) claimed, the global use of ELF in business system is not a negotiation; its adoption will be indispensable. However, ELF notion has been criticized for several reasons.

The concept of ELF is distinct from other varieties of English since it has its own characters and this may be the reason that ELF has been exposed to criticism by a number of researchers within the field of English studies. It has been argued that ELF is "monolithic", in other words, it represents only one model of English speakers from the Expanding Circle (Jenkins, 2009; Park & Wee, 2011). On the other hand, other varieties of English could be criticized for being monolithic that badly affects the identity of the 'Expanding Circle' speakers (Jenkins, 2009) because the World Englishes paradigm focuses more on Inner and Outer Circle speakers and less on Expanding Circle speakers (Seidlhofer, 2009). It is true that ELF focuses more on speakers from the Expanding Circle; however speakers from Inner and Outer Circles are also represented as communication may occur among all three circle's speakers (Jenkins, 2009). ELF has been also criticized for lacking any standard or codification, which means it does not have a system or base that any English language variant should have; otherwise errors will appear constantly, (Cogo & Jenkins, 2010; Jenkins, 2009; Park & Wee, 2011). There is no doubt that ELF can be distinguished from other varieties in many aspects such as pronunciation, use of words and code-mixing, nevertheless, nonstandard form seems to appear in a wide range of English varieties including British "vernaculars", which puts them within the same tent with ELF (Kirkpatrick, 2010). One case is that of omitting the plural indicator from nouns of measurement (e.g., *she runs for two miles*). Champer also lists several non-standard forms that are shared across all varieties of English such as double negative in a sentence and deletion of the verb 'be' when it should be used (Champer, 2004, as cited in Kirkpatrick, 2010). Therefore, as mentioned earlier, ELF is similar to other English varieties in exhibiting forms of usage that would be deemed grammatical errors according to Standard English.

This is proved when House (1999 as cited in Kaur, 2011) could not find any direct evidence that could directly connect the misunderstanding among non-native speakers to the variety of culture among them. None of ELF speakers speak English as a mother-tongue and that might be the reason behind the difficulty to accept or consider ELF as one of English varieties, (Seidlhofer, 2009). However, this is what makes ELF unique, as Firth points out: "-it is not that ELF is too variable to be a variety: rather, it is that variability is itself one of ELF's principle characters" (Firth, 2009, as cited in Cogo & Jenkins, 2010).

ELF deserves to be called a variety of the English language because it meets the conditions of providing effective interaction and understanding among English speakers. The crucial role of ELF in international business and technology cannot be denied. The similarities between ELF and other varieties of English regarding Standard English and the unique characters of ELF strongly support the argument that ELF should be considered as one of the varieties of English language. More studies of ELF might be required to investigate the negative points raised by some researchers of English studies.

The Status and Role of English as an International Language

In the discussion of the status and role of English as an international language, various perspectives have been expressed. Several authors, notably Pennycook (1994) and Phillipson (1992), have spoken from a socio-political perspective. Phillipson sees the dominance of English and ELT as "linguistic imperialism", claiming that the English speaking countries impose their cultural values and military and economic power upon the 'Other' through ELT. As a result, the notion of the language is closely tied to its native speakers and the core native speaker countries. However, a global view of ELT that appreciates how widely English has spread and how diverse it has become in character discourages narrow identification of English mainly with native speakers. Understanding of the global nature of the language has not led to specific linguistic descriptions. Seidlhofer (2001) describes this state of affairs as a 'conceptual gap', meaning an absence of scholarly description and recognition of language that prevents us from acknowledging speakers of ELF as language users in their own right. The call for a research agenda which may help accord ELF a central place in description alongside the notions of English as a native language has been strongly supported by a number of researchers, such as House (1999), Jenkins (2000, 2002, 2004). An important contribution, in this respect, however, is provided in Brutt - Griffler 's (2002) book *World English*. Here the account of the global spread of English is considered to be becoming apprehensive , persuasive, highly detailed and to have more "explanatory power" than other accounts available (Seidlhofer, 2004). The explanatory framework for the use of English worldwide takes into account current global issues. A number of reasons for, and consequences of, the spread of English internationally are encapsulated in her descriptions of " econocultural grounds" (Brutt-Griffler, 2002). The framework also "attempts to overcome the limitations of the existing theoretical perspectives and to subsume various strands in the development of World English under one unifying theoretical framework" (Brutt-Griffler, 2002, p. 109). In this explanatory framework, four central features of the development of English are demonstrated, as follows:

1. English spreads as it performs an econocultural function on a global scale. World English in fact is the product of the development of a world market as well as global developments in the areas of business, science and technology, culture, and media.
2. World English is increasingly used by people of various classes in the society, not just by the socioeconomically elite groups. The language is used for a variety of purposes by its participants who have various levels of fluency.
3. World English establishes itself as a consequence of the stabilisation of bilingualism which can be gained through the coexistence of this world language alongside other languages in multilingual contexts. In other words, World English contributes to multilingualism rather than undermines it.
4. World English spreads because many people learn it, rather than being spread by speakers of English transmitting it to the other areas. So "new varieties are created and unity in the world language is maintained". (Brutt-Griffler, 2002)

Clearly, Brutt-Griffler (2002) elaborations on the development of the language challenge the assumptions of "linguistic imperialism" made by Phillipson (1992). In her counter argument, Brutt- Griffler (2002) points out that although imperialism has contributed to framing the "econocultural system" which formed the basis for development of English as a world language, and it does not constitute by any means the whole of its necessary conditions put differently, while we can assume that imperialism facilitated the development of the language as the world language; it would be false to believe that native speakers have all the responsibility for this spread of English. Such a standpoint is strongly supported by Pennycook (1994) who asserts that "it is important not to assume a deterministic relationship" between imperialism and English spread. In direct contrast to the imperialist perspectives, Brutt-Griffler (2002) emphasises that the language is "appropriated" by people at large who play active roles as agents in its spread. This view has significant implications for the description of ELF interactions in general and in the business context in particular.

Another relevant argument at this point is that it is insufficient just to conceive of ELF as a shared language; to change attitudes towards ELF it is necessary and also feasible to construct a descriptive and pedagogic model for its teaching and use (Seidlhofer, 2001). The elaboration of such a model requires an investigation of the forms of language used by different participants in a variety of contexts, including ELF settings. A potential model must also provide comprehensive and reliable descriptions of salient features of the language to provide a sound descriptive basis for actual language use. ELF, with its distinctive features, may become firmly established in people's minds alongside English as a native language. Empirical work on various levels of linguistic descriptions has been conducted with varying objectives from case to case (Seidlhofer, 2001, 2004). This accumulating body of work has been leading to a better understanding of the nature of ELF, and is at least having a positive impact on its recognition as a global language. However, it is beyond the scope of the present chapter to elaborate on the findings of these studies. A focus on distinctive features of ELF integration and the use of ELF in business contexts is more relevant.

English as a Language for Communication

In an attempt to define a lingua franca from a formal perspective, House (2003) asks whether ELF is a language for specific purposes, a pidgin, or a type of inter language and how it differs from native English. In answering to these questions, she argues that ELF is neither a language for specific purposes nor a pidgin because there are no signs of marginal or special varieties of the language. In different situations in which ELF is used for different purposes, a great deal of grammatical and lexical material is used in common. On this point, House refers to Kachru's ideas that ELF is not a restricted code, but a language that has a comprehensive showing of full linguistic characteristics and provides a wide functional range (Kachru, 1997 cited in House, 2003).

With regard to the interlanguage aspect, House emphasises that ELF interactions are not considered to be conducted with a view to an ideal English norm and that a lingua franca speaker may not be fully competent in his/her language use. At the same time, the object of inquiry for ELF is not concerned with the psycholinguistic perspective, which looks at the development of an 'in-between system' inside a speaker's mind as English competence is acquired. As Firth (1996) observes, ELF discourse belongs to interactions between non-natives, and has been investigated with a focus on the negotiation of meaning between ELF participants having varying linguistic resources. This approach, therefore, is associated with social language-use rather than individual linguistic aspects. As an ELF researcher in this perspective, one attempts to conceptualise the participant simply as a "*language user* whose realworld interactions are deserving of unprejudiced *description* rather than as a person conceived *a priori* to be the possessor of incomplete or deficient communicative competence, putatively striving for the 'target' competence of an idealized 'native speaker'." (Firth, 1996, p. 241).

To argue for the distinctive functions of ELF discourse, House (2003) refers to several empirical studies on ELF talk. Typical among these, she notes, are the work by Firth (1996), Haegeman (2002), Lesznyák (2002), and Meierkord (2002). Conclusions from these studies reveal the fluid nature of ELF talk in terms of the norms that are operative in the interactive process. Since ELF speakers possess different culturally-based knowledge frames, potential difficulties may arise as their talk proceeds. However, according to House (2003), the authors of these studies stress that ELF participants seem to strive for communicative success and efficiency through their cooperation in constructing discourse. They tend to normalise their trouble sources rather than handle them explicitly through the techniques of speech repairs. Such procedures in fact help ELF interactions to be meaningful and ordinary (House, 2003). With this function to facilitate interactions, ELF is described as a language filled with a repertoire of different communicative instruments an individual has at his/her disposal, which could be a useful and versatile tool serving its purpose as a language for communication (House, 2003).

Thus, ELF can be regarded as a language for communication which is a useful instrument for fulfilling certain functions in human experience.

House (2003) describes this view of language as one "uniting both cognitive-individual and social foci on language" (p. 559). And accordingly, in ELF use "speakers must continuously work out a joint basis for their interactions, locally construing and intersubjectively ratifying meanings" (p. 559).

In addition, in using ELF, speakers are unlikely to regard it as a language for identity marking but simply a transactional language for communicative purposes and advantage. It is usually an individual's L1language that helps define the L1 group and its members as core determinants of identity. ELF, on the other hand, which is not a national language but merely a functional tool enables communication with others who do not speak one's own L1, does not otherwise identify groups of ELF speakers. Kramsch (2002) illustrates the distinction between using language for communicative purposes and using it as a way to show one's identity through an example of an autobiography of a native speaker of Vietnamese. This speaker revealed affective-emotive elements as part of his/her identity in speaking L1:

A similar position is also taken in the discussion of languages used as lingua franca in Crystal (1997), who argues that 'World Standard Spoken English' is an additional form of English which is accessible to speakers around the globe to communicate with people from other countries. Crystal does not support the assumption that World Standard Spoken English will be used to convey emotional ties or identity. This view of the appropriation of English for international communication rather than a symbol of national supremacy is also supported increasingly by a number of researchers in Europe and North America (Brutt-Griffler, 2002; Seidlhofer, 2001), and notably by scholars in Outer Circle countries, for example Chew (1999) in Singapore and Bisong (1995) in Nigeria. It is communication needs that require and also affect the way people learn and use the language. Seidlhofer (2009) argues that this emerging perspective marks the beginning of a new era in the study of the global use of English where the concept of 'linguistic imperialism' seems to be replaced by 'functional realism'.

ELF speakers are not primarily concerned with emulating the way native speakers use their mother- tongue within their own communities, nor with socio- psychological and ideological issues. Instead, the central concerns for this domain are efficiency, relevance and economy in language learning and language use. The reasons why the linguistic imperialism school has had little impact on mainstream ELT are rather obvious: people need and want to learn English whatever the ideological baggage that comes with it...(Seidlhofer, 2000, cited in Rogerson-Revell, 2007, p. 108).

In light of the above discussion, the inference is that the dichotomy between language for identity and language for communication has significant implications for any investigation of language-use in ELF interactions. Moreover it affirms House's (2003) idea that ELF research is necessary if it is "to match and indeed provide some guidance for, the global use of English as a language for communication" (p. 571). The origin and result of ELF acquisition and use involve social processes associated with the socio-historical condition of language -spread. Suitable models of research in language-use therefore must take into account the significance of social processes that affect individual language performance. House seems to be correct in stressing that it is imperative to rethink the linguistic norms against which an ELF speaker's discourse competence is to be measured. In addition, because ELF users may never intend to consider native speaker pragmatics as a target to achieve, and native speakers may not admit non-native speakers' discourse as compatible with the native norm, there is no clear-cut set of criteria for measuring performance of all ELF speakers (Kasper, 1984). In a given situation, the socio-cultural and historical conditions in which the language is used as well as the specific goals for interaction should be taken into account for a better understanding of how language works. Such a perspective of ELF interactions is pertinent to this research, which investigates the various factors influencing English language acquisition in the sub-continent as it continues to grow into being the largest English speaking nation in the world (Kasper, 1984).

Recent research into the use of English in business contexts has covered all three situations in which the language is used, namely English as a first-language, as a second-language and as a foreign language, (Nickerson, 2005). For example, Charles (1996) investigated the organisation and rhetoric of sales negotiation using data generated by English native speakers. Most European-based research has involved speakers of English as a foreign language; typical among such studies are the work by Connor et al. (1997) in application letters and Louhiala - Salminen, Charles and Kankaanranta (2005a) in written business communication within two large Nordic corporations in non-English speaking countries.

The term BELF (Business ELF) is used by Louhiala -Salminen et al. (2005) to refer only to the use of English for business purposes between speakers whose mother-tongue is not English.However, the international business arena today is growing in complexity due to numerous factors, including the spread of information technology, the rising incidence of mergers and acquisitions worldwide, the growth of global markets and the increasing interdependence among businesses. As a result, the international business community includes a multinational workforce moving and communicating across borders, which give rise to a variety of situations in which English is used simultaneously as a first, second and foreign language (Louhiala- Salminen, Charles, & Kankaanranta, 2005b). Thus, English discourse constructed in real-life business situations seems to be far more complicated than what some studies suggest. The term English for International Business reflects the more liberal and flexible nature of current international use of English for business purposes. Clearly the English language evolved as a language of communication for various reasons of which business communication in the international arena was predominant with other factors such as job opportunities, educational prospects, fashion trends and media also playing major roles.

The use of English as a lingua franca with a focus on its growth in the communication and business context has been discussed in detail. The international spread of English, its historical causes and consequences have also been analysed. It also presented a theoretical perspective which challenged simplistic accounts of 'linguistic imperialism' and offered a more nuanced understanding of the nature of international English. Seidlhofer (2001) raised a number of questions but justified his position and argument with "it is early days yet and all these questions will have to be formulated and addressed with care and circumspection" (p. 147). Findings from these studies have shed light on some of the language issues present in international communication and also on the difficulties and frustrations that may result. Besides uncovering communication issues, these studies are useful in developing awareness of some of the strategies that can be used to overcome communicative difficulties. It seems that the use of English as a lingua franca in the international arena is much more complicated than research has suggested. Generally, the historical, geographical, economic and political conditions influence how English has been spreading to different continents worldwide. These conditions also decide whether English is maintained and promoted in each case. As business and various forms of trade has led to globalisation and the development of ELF, these conditions have direct impacts on how the relationships between the ELF and the native languages are going to involve.

Chapter - 4

India and the English Language

The Largest English Speaking Nation

The second most spoken language in the world after Chinese Mandarin, 'English' plays an essential role in increasing opportunity in every sphere of life all over the world (BBC, 2013). English as a language provides extensive access to information by which whole populations can gain knowledge, and develop the skills and networks necessary for mankind's future progress and prosperity. English is the common language with which most of the globe shares knowledge and ideas to generate relationships which grow beyond a simple deal or contract. It has spread more widely than any other language and it is a language not just of commerce but of conversation. It enables individuals to explore cultural differences and to produce the faith, hope, conviction and understanding which are essential in negotiating and harmonizing our common future. At present English can be argued to be the language showing the most proven capacity for unifying the globe.

It might be difficult for the native speaker of English to digest the fact that currently, India is in its pathway towards becoming the largest English speaking nation in the world. As early as in 2005, David Crystal, the internationally renowned linguist reported on the dynamic varieties of English evolving on the Indian sub- continent in his interview to ABC as "India currently has a special place in the English language record books, as the country with the largest English-speaking population in the world"(Crystal, 2005, p. 1). Despite not having a long history of English speaking, Graddol (2010) feels that India commands a strong lead in the teaching and learning of English, yet increasing access to opportunity to learn English remains a significant challenge. The challenge of taking what is still the language of the elite and turning it into an instrument for modern communication for the masses is multifaceted and daunting. Modern India boasts a talented pool of young, adept users of the English language, who can transform Indian society and who can provide the required momentum for its growth, even in a globally competitive, financially unstable environment (Graddol, 2006).

This study aims to contribute to the development of English language teaching and learning in India and to develop a better understanding of the issues facing it while drawing on the experience of a wide range of educators from India. Some controversies that prevail in the language and linguistics area are the basic assumption that considering India as the largest English speaking nation in the worlds is a myth. In the teaching of English as an International Language (EIL), and as a lingua franca there are certain underlying assumptions which this study evaluates from different perspectives and the problems that are highlighted. An attempt is made to show that the new approach to learning the English Language cannot lead us to any secure place supposed to be characteristically distinct from its predecessors. There are various factors influencing English language growth in the subcontinent and this research identifies them and explores the reason why they are occurring and analyses the factors influencing them through the viewpoint of educators from various disciplines, specialisations, age groups, cultures, demographics and besides it tries to fathom what is the future of English in India.

English as a Link Language

India is one of the emerging superpowers of the world, together with China and Brazil, but what sets it apart from its major economic and strategic competitors such as Japan, China and Brazil is its status as the second largest English-speaking nation in the world (The Times of India, 11 Nov 2005). This is a significant advantage for India especially in a world where English is the lingua franca. It has the second largest population of "fluent English" speakers, second only to the U.S., and is expected to have the largest in coming decades. At the same time, in India, English has a status of "link language" (Daniel, 2007), but it is the most important language of India, after Hindi, it is the most commonly spoken language in India and probably the most read and written language in India.

English is the state language of two states in Eastern India, Meghalaya and Nagaland, and it is the main medium of instruction in most institutions of higher learning at the postgraduate level. It is taught as a second-language in almost all the states in India. Out of the seven major daily newspapers in India that have been in existence for over one hundred years, four are published in English which are *The Times Of India,* Bombay (1850); *The Pioneer*, Lucknow (1865); *The Mail,* Madras *(1867)* and *Amrita Bazaar Patrika,* Calcutta *(1868)* (Kachru, 1983). Among, the most circulated Newspapers 'The Hindu', 'The Indian Express' and Deccan Chronicle' are English dailies. As a link language English acts as a bridging language between the various other languages spoken between the diverse ethnic masses and minorities. India has 22 officially recognised languages in conjunction with around 33 other languages and 2000 dialects that have been identified in India (indiastat.com, 2012). Hindi, in the Devanagari script is the official language of the Federal Central government of India but English is an associate official language. Sanskrit, the classical language of India, represents the highest achievement of the Indo- Aryan Languages. English is accepted nationally while other languages and dialects are accepted in particular regions only. The officially recognized languages are statespecific, spoken only by people of a particular state. The term 'officially recognized' here denotes those languages that may be used in government examinations. In reality, only Hindi and English are nationally used languages. English has gained tremendous importance in the Indian education system and economy. Most of the schools, especially in the cities and towns, use English as a first-language for all communication, written and spoken. A person travelling outside his state is unable to communicate unless he knows the language of the state he is in or the English language. English therefore assumes the status of 'link language' for the common

India and Written English

India is the third largest book producing country after the US and the UK, and the majority of these books are published in English (Khokhar, 2006). Creative writing in English has been an integral part of the Indian literary tradition for many years. Indian English has been used widely by several writers who have been able to successfully use the language to create rich and invigorating literature. India is rich with tastes, sounds, and sights that are any writer's dream and stylistic influence from local languages is a particular feature of Indian literature in English. Many perceive English as having released the local languages from rigid classical traditions that could be an obstacle while writing (Khokhar, 2006). Indian writers in English have truly showcased India to the world, helping understanding of the country, increasingly as the range of Indian English has grown and no longer reflects and represents only western concepts of literary creativity. The language as established itself in the country and has acquired its own independent identity. David Crystal (2008) states that collections of Indian English vocabulary have been around for more than a century. Hobson-Jobson was the first, published in 1886. It is largely of historical interest now, and there have been attempts to revise and update it, such as Hanklin-Janklin, (compiled by Nigel Hanklin, Banyan Books, 2004), but no dictionary has yet catalogued the extraordinary stylistic range and regional diversity of Indian English (Crystal, 2008).

India and Commercial English

With the number of foreign investors flocking to India and the growth of outsourcing, English has come to play a key role in professional relationships between foreign and Indian companies, (Khokhar, 2006). Familiarity with the differences between American and British English has definitely grown since business communication must be carried out according to the language style with which a client is comfortable. Though many may perceive the accent, terminology, and conversational style of the hybrid forms of business English as peculiar, in reality they are just different forms of English that cannot simply be equated with American or British English, (Khokhar, 2006). Indians are familiar with both types of English, but Indian English has acquired its own character in a country which is a melting pot of various cultures, people, and traditions. It is a linguistic bridge between the major first language dialects of the world, such as British and American English, and the major foreign language varieties, such as those emerging in China and Japan. China is the closest competitor for the English speaking record with some two hundred and twenty million speakers of English, but China does not have the pervasive English linguistic environment encountered in India; nor does it have the strength of linguistic tradition that provides multiple continuities with the rest of the English speaking world (Crystal, 2004).

India is described as a technology superpower and considered the 'World's Office' by leading in the Services Industry (Dossani, 2003). This is mainly due to India's development of a large pool of highly skilled, low cost, English speaking workers in the knowledge economy. Due to its high birth rate India has a young population compared to most aging nations: approximately sixty percent of its population are below the age of thirty (Khanna, 2007). In addition, declining fertility is beginning to reduce the youth dependency rate, which may produce a demographic dividend.

In the coming decades, while some of the powerful nations witness a decrease in workforce, India is expected to experience an increase. However the country suffers from many economic, social, and political problems that it must overcome before it can be considered a superpower. Whether India's being the largest English speaking nation in the world will benefit the nation as a whole or tend to divide an affluent, educated society from the underprivileged, economically weaker sections of society is yet to be analysed.

The Social Context

In many ways life in India today features terrible hardship and inequity. In 2005, more than ten thousand desperate Indian farmers killed themselves, most often by swallowing pesticides, because they could not meet their debts. India exports cereals, but more than fifty percent of its children are malnourished. Forty percent of Indians can neither read nor write, while only ten percent of Chinese are illiterate, and India ranks 126th on the UN Human Development Index, well below China in 81st place (Bulard, 2007). Unfortunately for those whose suffering is reflected in these dire statistics, the few corrective measures that the government has attempted have often been undermined by wide scale corruption. Neither the government nor the upper classes seem concerned about the divide that separates the majority of India from the sixty to seventy million people (the affluent five to six percent of the population) who have achieved a standard of living comparable to that in Europe (Bulard, 2007). Shashi Tharoor, a prominent Indian politician and a member of parliament (MP) from one of the southern states in India, states,

"We must do something for the other India . . . We must invest in hardware roads, ports and airports, all in a pitiful state, but also in software, the human beings to whom we must give what they need. It is a question of civilisation. Wholesale exclusion is the vulnerable point of India, which seeks to present itself as the largest democracy in the world" (Bulard, 2007).

The Geopolitics of Language

The race has begun between the Elephant and the Dragon and as the economist Amartya Sen has suggested, "the earliest Sino-Indian relations were initiated by trade rather than Buddhism" (Bulard, 2007). India does not yet seem capable of any spectacular strategic initiative. The writer Sunil Khilnani said, shrewdly: "We have become enamoured of the idea that we are soon to become a permanent invitee to the perpetual soiree of great powers, and so must dust ourselves off and dress for the part . . . But we need to deliberate over what the role should be, and how we can most effectively achieve it" (Bulard, 2007). India's dream of national strength and wealth is now a reality: its superpower status is indisputable. However the country suffers from many economic, social, and political problems that it must overcome before it can be considered a superpower. . Yet it is rejecting cultural uniformity, writes Pankaj Mishra. It will be a long time before India is fully modern as orthodox cultural values that continue through centuries will be hard to untie and this may be a very good thing for the society at large. Many different worlds coexist in India, and together they keep unifying and homogenising influences in check (Mishra, 2006). It may be a long time before India is fully modern as the centuries old orthodox cultural ties gradually flex and loosen allowing Indian society at large to come into its own.

This leads to the question; do Indians appreciate their own achievements in acquiring English? Ultimately, it would seem that they do. It has been said that Indians have made English into a native language with its own linguistic and cultural ecologies and socio-cultural contexts. English newspapers are published in every part of India; even in 1978 the English language press represented 19.5% of the Indian Press (Kachru, 1983). In the middle-class educated section of the population there is a strong widespread parental pressure for English medium education, as well as a readiness of such schools to accept students usually without proselytizing, but also without compromising, and often needing the numbers to survive. These English acquiring communities have had an influence far beyond their size, first within the British Empire, then because of a disproportionate influence on education, social life, and career prospects in post- imperial nation-states. The largest such community has been an Anglo-Indian one whose mainly Protestant school networks have served as a homogenizing factor in India from North to South, and contributed to a more or less national style of speech, often identified as the medium of an envied national elite (McArthurr, 2003).

Evolving India

The evolution of language loyalties is superficially linked to political expressions through the medium of organised associations and their affiliations to political processes and agendas intentionally and unintentionally (Dasgupta, 1970). Predominantly loyalties are based on ethnicity, religion, culture and gender; the love of individual human beings for their language is as old as history, that is to say, it is built into their genetic make-up, with a hunger and passion inherent and unfathomable. The invention of printing played a very crucial role, which hastened the spread of education to the middle and lower classes in society. Subsequently, Humanism and the resulting reformation with the increasing participation of the general population in local and national politics and policies has laid the way for the decisive placing of a premium on language loyalties and its expression in nationalism (Dasgupta, 1970).

The developments in European society, throughout the centuries had gradually persuaded romantic thinkers to believe "that language is the most important identifying characteristic of people and therefore it should be the obvious criterion of national political boundaries" (Dasgupta, 1970). The present era of scholars and linguists tend to reject such thinking since the vast complexity of the relationship between language and political community needs to be factored into an ever evolving, shifting, uncertain, problematic nature of language. In view of the fact that people in a nation are constantly migrating, immigrating and changing the face of a nation, the relationship between language and national identity can be extremely tenuous. The best illustration has to be from Australia, a society whose people are from a rich variety of cultural, ethnic, linguistic and religious backgrounds. Aboriginal and Torres Strait Islander people have inhabited Australia for tens of thousands of years. However, most Australians are immigrants or the descendants of immigrants who arrived during the past two centuries from more than 200 countries. As per the 2011 Census, one in four Australian is born overseas and the overseas born people in Australia though predominantly from North-West Europe, Southern and Eastern Europe currently the exodus is mostly from South-East Asia, Oceania, North-East Asia, Southern and Central Asia, North Africa, the Middle East, Sub-Saharan Africa and the Americas. The biggest increases in population of overseas born people between the 2001 and 2006 Censuses were from bChina (64, 000), India (52, 000), New Zealand (34, 000) and South Africa (25, 000). Of the country-of-birth groups that had a population of more than 1000 at the 2006 Census, the fastest growing were people from Liberia (up 1240 percent from the 2001 Census), Sierra Leone (up 437 percent) and the Sudan (up 288 percent) (Australian Bureau of Statistics, 2010).

Consequently, in Europe and various other parts of the world, like the U.S.A., the transformation of traditional societies into modern political communities has always been accompanied by corresponding linguistic modernization, an intergroup phenomenon characterized by peculiar extremes of internal linguistic diversity. In such societies administration, religious affairs, literary activity and day to day ordinary communication activities are carried out in different languages, as is predominantly common in India and various parts of Asia even in the twenty first century. Given that, in a traditional society classical or foreign languages are employed for administrative purposes as is widespread in India whereas the local population generally speak a variety of official and unofficial languages and dialects in which some may sometimes be illiterate in one while literate in the other. On the other hand, with the trend towards modernity, literacy and education, the gap between the literary language and the popular native language gradually diminishes, (Dasgupta, 1970).

The process of linguistic modernisation and the gradual evolution of English into a globalised standard language started its emergence in Europe from the mid part of the eleventh century, saw a considerable hastening of the process in the nineteenth century and arrived at a dramatic culmination towards the late twenty century, predominantly in contemporary modern Asia and Africa. The seed was sown for the standardisation of English as a global language because the distance between its variants were diminishing, though this depended on individual nation's political situation, intellectual initiatives, forms of national consciousness and language loyalties linked to patriotism. This standardisation rang the death knell of the dominance of classical languages and provided a new basis for linguistic unity between the elite and the masses within national political communities, (Dasgupta, 1970).

In countries like India, Pakistan, Sri Lanka and Malaysia a variety of languages existed with their own substantial traditions. The lack of an assured single dominant national language generated acute language rivalry and, in political terms, a desire for national independence from being under colonial regimes. Gradually the benefits of accepting English as the standard language overcame indigenous language rivalry, for it became apparent that improved literacy growth, and expansion of education also helped improve communication in trade, economics and commerce, all of which was for the future betterment of the country as a whole. In spite of the convenience, rationality and efficiency, they are not the decisive criteria in language policies decision making process which are more from the political perspective than from a comfortable technical viewpoint.

The choice of a national language in India was very complicated and potentially explosive linguistic issue, especially when no single language could claim an overwhelming dominance over the others. A concrete account of Indian Languages was prepared by George Grierson in his monumental study published in nineteen volumes from 1903 to 1928. This sophisticated analysis revealed the "existence of 179 languages and 544 dialects in undivided India and the 1961 census of India mentions 1,652, Mother Tongues" (Dasgupta, 1970, p. 33). The Indian Census Organization of 1991 claims that there are a total of 114 languages and 216 mother tongues, 18 scheduled languages and 96 not specified in the schedule (Mallikarjun, 2001). To add to the conflict a number of regional languages are significant and have distinct literary heritage and religious identification, for example the Urdu spoken by the Muslims, Punjabi by the Sikhs, Hindi by the Hindus and English by the elite and Christians in India. Another complicating factor is the cultural, religious and political alliances with neighbouring nations that creates political suspicion, as in Urdu being spoken by the Muslims in Pakistan and Tamil being spoken by the Hindu Tamils in Sri Lanka and Malaysia the Tamils in Tamil Nadu, the southernmost state in India.

There are 15 national languages recognized by the Indian constitution and these are spoken in over 1600 dialects. The national or official languages are Assamese, Bengali, Gujarati, Hindi, Kannada, Kashmiri, Malayalam, Marathi, Oriya, Panjabi, Sanskrit, Sindhi, Tamil, Telugu, Urdu and English (Associate Official). An estimated 850 languages are in daily use in India; the nation has a wide variety of local languages and, constitutionally, the state boundaries have been drawn on linguistic lines. Though India gives an impression of multilingualism, its great diversity and population creates monolingualism, for out of a 439 million people only 30 million are revealed in 1961 census as bilingual (Dasgupta, 1970). Inevitably, although 223,000 people have stated English as their mother tongue, eleven million had declared knowing English, revealing English to be the most widely known second-language in India, with the use of English universally and transactionally being very extensive since it provided more opportunities in every arena (Dasgupta, 1970).

For theoretical and analytical purposes the 'UNESCO' definition of 'official language' as "an accepted language of administration as well as a means of communication between the government and the governed" (Dasgupta, 1970, p. 37) is very relevant for the Indian scenario. The official language was not the common language of the people of that nation but inevitably evolved into one with time. In spite of common politicians referring to Hindi as the 'national language', the elite and wise fathers of the Indian constitution were very explicit in avoiding the notion of common or national language but referred more to them as regional or state languages and to English as a link language.

Language Survey Reveals Diversity

There are over 780 languages and 66 different scripts in India. Arunachal Pradesh is the richest among the States with 90 languages. These findings and more, are set to come to light with the publication of a baseline survey of Indian languages by the People's Linguistic Survey of India. Comprising 50 volumes, the survey would be published between September 2013 and December 2014. Work on the independent survey, now in its final stages, has so far thrown up interesting results. For instance, it has been found the West Bengal has the highest number of scripts at nine (The Peoples Linguistic Survey of India, 2017).

Researchers found that Assam with 55 languages, Gujarat 48, Maharashtra 39 and West Bengal 38 are among the most linguistically diverse States. "As per the 2011 Census, there are about 122 languages spoken by more than 10,000 people. Of them 22 are the scheduled languages. Other than the 122 languages, the survey has come up with languages that are spoken by less than 10,000 people many from tribal areas, nomadic communities and from the interiors of North Eastern part of the country" (The Peoples Linguistic Survey of India, 2017). The survey, has revealed that the north eastern parts of the country have one of the highest per capita language densities in the world. Consequently, the difficult topography of the region and the history of the tribal communities could have led to such a situation. Since Hindi in South India was viewed suspiciously as the symbol of North Indian domination, the non-Hindi speaking states felt that they would miss out on equal opportunities. At the same time the Hindi area is spread over several states, in contrast to the other state languages which are confined to their individual states. The linguistic bond of such an extended belt of states, altogether of immense size and population tended to give the impression that the Hindi area represented the heartland of the nation India since the significance of this area in terms of population and physical area is immense, (Dasgupta, 1970) as represented in Table No. 1.

Other than political concerns the other major consideration was that the literacy rates in the major Hindi states have always been significantly lower than those of the other major non Hindi speaking states. This highlighted the issue of educational development being much lower in the Hindi belt than the non Hindi speaking states. The below tables 1, 2 and 3 clearly analyse and revel in a simplistic and comprehensive form the literacy levels in Hindi belt & non Hindi belt through a comparison of the last 50 to 100 years.

Table No. 1: Percentage of Literacy Rates by Sex in India Hindi Speaking States,

Population, Area, % Population Literate

Percentage of Literacy Rates by Sex in India (1901, 1911, 1921, 1931, 1941, 1951, 1961, 1971, 1981, 1991 and 2001)

Year	*Age Group*	*Persons*	*Males*	*Females*	*Rural*	*Urban*	*Male- Female Gap in Literacy Rate*
1901+		5.39	9.83	0.60	-	-	9.23
1911+	All Population All	5.92	10.56	1.05	-	-	9.51
1921+	Population All	7.16	12.21	1.81	-	-	10.40
1931+	Population All	9.50	15.59	2.93	-	-	12.66
1941+	Population All	16.10	24.90	7.30	-	-	17.60
1951	Population 5	18.33	27.16	8.86	12.10	34.59	18.30
	and above	28.31	40.40 1	5.34	22.46	54.43	25.06
1961	5 and above	34.45	45.95	21.97	27.89	60.22	23.98
1971	5 and above	43.56	56.37	29.75			
1981	7 and above	(41.42)	(53.45)	(28.46)	36.09	67.34	26.65
1991	7 and above	52.21	63.86	39.42	44.69	73.09	24.84
2001#	-	64.8	75.3	53.7	-	-	21.59

Source: Human Resource Development, Govt. of India (Indiastats, 2012).

Note: + : For Undivided India.- : Not Available.: The 1981 rates exclude Assam where the 1981 census could not be conducted. The 1991 Census rates exclude Jammu & Kashmir where the 1991 Census was not conducted. The Literacy rates for India have been worked out by excluding the population and number of literates of areas affected by natural calamities of Gujarat and Himachal Pradesh. Literacy rate for 1951. 1961 & 1971 relate to population aged five years and above. The rates for the years 1981, 1991 & 2001 relate to the population aged seven years and above. The literacy rates for the population aged five years and above in 1981 have been shown in brackets.

Table No. 2: Crude Literacy Rates by Sex in India

Crude Literacy Rates by Sex in India (1901, 1911, 1921, 1931, 1941, 1951, 1961, 1971, 1981, 1991, 2001 and 2004-2005)

Crude Literacy Rates by Sex in India (1901, 1911, 1921, 1931, 1941, 1951, 1961, 1971, 1981, 1991, 2001 and 2004-2005)						
Census Year	*Crude Literacy Rate Points (% age)*			*Change in Percent Points*		
	Persons	*Males*	*Females*	*Persons*	*Males*	*Females*
1901	5.35	9.83	0.60	-	-	-
1911	5.92	10.56	1.05	0.57	0.73	0.45
1921	7.16	12.21	1.81	1.24	1.65	0.76

(Contd...)

1931	9.50	15.59	2.93	2.34	3.38	1.12
1941	16.10	24.90	7.30	6.60	9.31	4.37
1951	16.67	24.95	7.93	0.57	0.05	0.63
1961	24.02	34.44	12.95	7.35	9.49	5.02
1971	29.45	39.45	18.69	5.43	5.01	5.74
1981	36.23	46.89	24.82	6.78	7.44	6.13
1991	42.84	52.74	32.17	6.61	5.85	7.35
2001	54.51	63.24	45.15	11.67	10.50	12.98
2004-05*	63.60	78.00	51.10	9.09	14.76	5.95

Source: Human Resource Development, Govt. of India (Indiastats, 2012).
Note:*: NSS 61st Round Survey Report No. 517, 2004-2005.

Table No. 3: State-wise Top Ten and Bottom Ten Districts According to Literacy Rates by Sex in India

Top Ten Districts of India

District	*States/UTs*	*Literacy Rate*
	Persons	
Aizawl	Mizoram	96.64
Serchhip	Mizoram	96.16
Kottayam	Kerala	95.90
Mahe	Pondicherry*	95.78
Pathanamthitta	Kerala	95.09
Alappuzha	Kerala	93.66
Ernakulam	Kerala	
Kannur	Kerala	92.80
Thrissur	Kerala	92.56
Kozhikode	Kerala	92.45
	Males	
Mahe	Pondicherry*	97.59
Kottayam	Kerala	97.41
Serchhip	Mizoram	97.24
Aizawl	Mizoram	97.20
Pathanamthitta	Kerala	96.62
Alappuzha	Kerala	96.42
Kannur	Kerala	96.38
Kozhikode	Kerala	96.30
Ernakulam	Kerala	95.95
Thrissur	Kerala	95.47

(*Contd...*)

Females		
Aizawl	Mizoram	96.06
Serchhip	Mizoram	95.02
Kottayam	Kerala	94.45
Mahe	Pondicherry*	94.23
Pathanamthitta	Kerala	93.71
Alappuzha	Kerala	91.14
Ernakulam	Kerala	90.96
Thrissur	Kerala	89.94
Champhai	Mizoram	89.64
Kannur	Kerala	89.57

Table No. 4 Bottom Ten Districts According to Literacy Rates by Sex in India

District	*States/UTs*	*Literacy Rate*
	Bottom Ten Districts of India	
	Persons	
Dantewada	Chhatisgarh	30.01
Pakaur	Jharkhand	30.54
Kishanganj	Bihar	31.02
Malkangiri	Orissa	31.26
Shravasti	Uttar Pradesh	34.25
Nabarangapur	Orissa	34.26
Balrampur	Uttar Pradesh	34.71
Araria	Bihar	34.94
Katihar	Bihar	35.29
Purnia	Bihar	35.51
	Males	
Dantewada	Chatisgarh	39.59
Pakaur	Jharkhand	40.19
Malkangiri	Orissa	41.21
Kishanganj	Bihar	42.80
Katihar	Bihar	45.51
Sheohar	Bihar	45.54
Purnia	Bihar	46.16
Balrampur	Uttar Pradesh	46.28
Bahraich	Uttar Pradesh	46.32
Araria	Bihar	46.50

(*Contd...*)

Females		
Kishanganj	Bihar	18.49
Shravasti	Uttar Pradesh	18.75
Pakaur	Jharkhand	20.44
Dantewada	Chhatisgarh	20.59

Source: Ministry of Human Resource Development, Govt. of India. (Indiastats, 2012).

Note: *Units The data of entire Kachchh district, Morvi, Maliya Miyana and Wankaner talukas of Rajkot district, Jodiya taluka of Jamnagar district of Gujarat State and entire Kinnaur district of Himachal Pradesh are not included where population enumeration of Census of India, 2001, could not be conducted due to natural calamity. Compiled from the statistics released by: Indiastats, 2012.

Year: Period of fiscal year in India is April to March, e.g. year shown as 1990-91 relates to April 1990 to March 1991.

Units: (a) 1 Lakh (or Lac) = 100000. (b) 1 Crore (or Cr.) = 10000000.

Some part of the footnotes/units may not be applicable for this table.

The data given in the three tables are exploratory and analytical by itself.

The total percentage of several scheduled languages in India is less than the percentage of speakers of English as mentioned by Kachru.(1983)

Assamese - 1.63%

Kannada - 3.96%

Kashmiri - 0.44%

Malayalam - 4.00%

Oriya - 3.62%

Punjabi - 3.00%

Sindhi - 0.31%

Such variations are due to functional, socio-cultural, educational and first language influence parameters with regional and geographical issues, (Kachru, 1983).

The new IT enabled economic revolution in India is transforming the traditional culture and standards of living of common Indian societies, and a key ingredient in this change seems to be the English language. As education and research bring new perspectives into a growing Indian economy, the English speaking 'talent pool' is being drained and the recruiter and the employee are beginning to think that perhaps not enough people in India speak English after all. Moreover, because of India's enormously complex inner structure, the unifying effect of English is greatly desired.

By many, India is seen as the most complex society in the world. It is defined as multifaceted not just because of its size, but because complexity seems to be manifested in a fractal pattern from national to local village level in every state in India. For example, throughout India, in the slums of the major metropolitan cities and in the starvation of the remote villages, a most abject poverty is visible, but everywhere this appears alongside contemporary, modernist building styles that Indians have adopted.

Many centuries of development, expansion and improvement of all kinds are visible in the cities of India and intermingled with this varied complexity of growth, the English language continues to keep pace with development and has been growing since its implantation during colonial times. Since its arrival on the subcontinent it has been debated whether English is more a burden or a liberation for the traditional orthodox Indian. Some have argued that the English language has created one of the biggest social divisions in an already divided society, between those who can speak English, and those who cannot (Graddol, 1996).

The Government of India has been very efficient in identifying the great social divide that is evolving in a nation already immeasurably culturally diverse. Despite the modern day literary divide being created between those who could speak English and those who can't, the government has recognised the importance of English for economic expansion, and has embarked on a program to make English universal.

The Government of India's eleventh Five Year Plan, which guides public sector policies during 2007–12, calls for a massive expansion of technical and vocational education, to provide the skills needed for the next phase of India's economic expansion. Finance Minister Pranab

Mukherjee, in the 2009 Budget speech has acclaimed that the: "The demographic advantage India has in terms of a large percentage of young population needs to be converted into a dynamic economic advantage by providing them the right education and skills"(Mukherjee, 2010).

In spite of the fact that the 'New Five Year Plans' has given a very high level of importance to improving the educational system in India, there is still a very significant shortage of teachers needed to implement effectively the English programs that are now being started in, or envisaged for, primary schools, secondary schools and vocational education centres. This consequently "is creating an environment of inequality of provision and inequality of learning outcomes" (Graddol, 2010). Graddol (2010) also considers the shortage of teachers specifically teaching English as one of the major reasons for the slow pace of progress nationally. Mere English medium education in the private sector is a contributing cause for the failure of the educational system for children do not and cannot learn English simply by being taught through English. An abrupt shift to an English medium school, which teaches all the subjects in English literally by translation without appropriate teaching of the language to the student and the teacher, causes educational failure. Attention should be given to bringing in sustained and direct instruction in English with the development of the mother tongue also remaining important. Poor English is consequently holding back Indian higher education since Indian universities continue to fall far short of rival countries in the quality of their teaching, research, and graduates. India would need more research universities to compete successfully as currently it has one of the lowest numbers of researchers per million as compared to developed and BRIC economies. A matter of even greater concern is the poor performance of the university sector in fostering research.

Table 5 : Numbers of researchers per million

Country	*Numbers of researchers per million*
India	119
Japan	5287
US	4484
China	663
Brazil	344
Russia	3319

Source: (Agarwal, 2006)

In depth and thorough surveys of English proficiency levels are needed as, without knowing more about the English proficiency levels of students and their teachers, it is impossible to make appropriate policy or plan for further training. The distribution of English skills across states, metropolitan cities and rural areas needs to be estimated to viably study the impact of particular interventions. India's language diversity is an important future resource hence schools need to focus on language development in all languages, including lesser used languages and minority languages. The Three Language Formula as presently implemented does not properly support multilingual development, hence new approaches are necessary and a diversity of approaches are required. Graddol (2010) argues that there is no single solution to the problem of low English proficiency a diversity of models is needed to fit local contexts. The Three Language Formula is not implemented by Hindi belt states. New states tried and failed in execution due to various practical problems.

India has come a long way from being a labour led economy and is on the verge of transforming itself into a major knowledge economy. This rapid economic growth has increased demand for skilled staff, both in services and manufacturing sectors. Reflecting this increase, there is a growing realization on the part of both government and business that the domestic supply of recruits with international standard skills is inadequate to meet the current and future demand. Addressing these issues would help the country overcome human capital challenges that could restrict future growth prospects. Over the next 10 years India is likely to emerge as the largest labour supplier and is currently at a stage of "demographic transition" where population growth is slowing down but the population of young people entering the labour force is growing and is expected to continue to do so. According to UN estimates, India will account for almost 26 percent of the increase in the global working age population over the next 10 years and is likely to contribute an additional 136 million people to the global labour pool (Agarwal, 2006).

The complexity of Indian society is profound, its diversity being subdivided by geography, religion, language, caste, age, gender, education and employment. Each cell in the complex matrix of Indian socioeconomic life grants its inhabitants a different experience of English, with distinct modes of learning and of use, and distinct degrees of empowerment or of marginalisation. Indian society now seems to be on an unstoppable trajectory of change, in a way which could not be foreseen even in the 1990s. But change is occurring at a very different pace in each sector of society, leading to major structural shifts in the pattern of inequality. The role of English in India is changing, triggered by a wider process of economic and social development which is increasing the number of people who know and use English. But speaking English is not a passive, accidental consequence of the change occurring in India; English language lies at the very heart of this change, enabling large sections of the economy to become more productive and at least a segment of society to become richer. Graddol (2010) asserts that, if access to English is unequal, then the gap between the rich and poor in India will widen. Such trends have certainly emerged in other developing countries, and the process appears to have begun in India with its heightened process of fast and radical changes. In some cases these are considered 'destiny' processes, cases in which the results can be predicted with confidence though the rate of progress and the overall timescale of the change are unclear.

Demographers such as Rajan, Sarma, & Mishra, 2003 are forecasting that overall the total population of India will continue to grow for some time, but that this growth is slowing. In the long term the general prediction is that it will stabilise and then is likelyto decrease. At the same time as this happens, India will ultimately move from being a young country, to one that suffers from some of the same social and economic problems now being experienced by developed countries with an ageing population (Rajan, Sarma, & Mishra, 2003). As history repeats itself, India has been and is already struggling to provide for its huge numbers of children, with only a small proportion of the population in productive work, creating the wealth and tax revenue to pay for education and social welfare. Nevertheless, in the future Graddol (2010, p18) predicts that the "problem will become the inverse: too few people in the productive workforce to support an ageing population. How long this transition will take is still a matter of debate, but it is likely to be at least half a century, and probably more".

Economist Professor Joseph Stiglitz (Biswas, 2006) argues that the "The difference between the economies of India and China has not so much to do with democracy, but the failure of India to invest adequately in education and health". Stiglitz warns that as a country develops, the structure of its employment must change. The dream of progress in India's agricultural sector is slowly emerging but still requires a substantial shift of people out of agriculture, allowing food production to become more efficient, mechanized, and based on different patterns of land ownership. This shift requires a huge investment in skills and training so that presently unskilled workers can take other jobs being created by the new economy. These jobs will require higher educational levels which will consequently pay better and provide families with greater security since higher pay scales require higher productivity to sustain the cycle of growth.

The highly controversial question currently being discussed amongst social theorists, politicians, academics and economists is this: What role does, or can, English play in this process? Growing the number of English speakers requires a hugeinvestment for both the country and for families and individuals. Graddol (2010, p.19) question is: "Will such an investment be rewarded, or does it represent a misdirection of resources? And if English is so important, how can the investment be best directed? Where are the weaknesses in the present 'pipeline' which produces English speakers?"

More English in the Indian social and environmental structure implies not just an economic rebalancing, but also a cultural one. Indian lifestyles are already changing, as the middle class grows in size and people change from simply trying to survive to becoming consumers. This means that English will probably play an increased role in private, as well as public, life. According to Graddol (2010 p20), the questions behind every Indian's mind now are these: "What does the increasing importance of English mean for the still unfinished project to make Hindi a national language? What does it mean for the status of regional languages? And what does it mean for the smaller, lesser used, unscheduled languages of India? Is the development road map one which leads inevitably to reduced linguistic diversity, or can India draw up a new map of its own, in which multilingualism becomes the goal, rather than English on its own?"

In the six decades since independence the nation of India has been in a continuous state of transition in most of its developing areas. In the area of language the transitions seem interlinked with influential factors entwined with the process of language acquisition, such as education, economy and population. Education is becoming viable for the common man in India, and as educational opportunities open avenues into economic prosperity the gap between the middle class and the poor is slowly shrinking as educational opportunities are opening avenues into economic prosperity.

With a young population forecast to continue to grow, possibly reaching over 2 billion before it stabilises early in the next century, the age structure will become more balanced allowing a greater proportion of the population to be of productive working age. (Indiastats, 2010). This will open up opportunities for the middle class, with disposable income to grow in size even in rural areas in spite of a greater percentage of people still living in cities. The transition will mean fewer people will be working in agriculture and more in the organised sector providing services as the domestic economy grows, becoming more important than the export sector. Economic prosperity will be the roots behind enrolment in education, up to the age of 14, approaching 100% with the quality of learning improving substantially as enrolments in higher education sharply increases. In addition, as spoken English, rather than just reading and writing, becomes a key skill, a majority of the population will become bilingual, with English as their second-language. (Graddol 2010)

The population of any nation will rise rapidly when mortality levels fall as a result of improved healthcare and nutrition. However, subsequently birth rates fall, a result partly of education and partly because of the family economic status and affordability. Eventually, the birth rate falls to the 'replacement rate' usually considered to be around 2.1 children per couple. Even at this stage, the total population keeps growing for decades, resulting from the 'wave' of younger people growing older. This process, from population increase, to stability, and then perhaps decline, is known as the 'demographic transition'. India's population is following this path: already increasing before independence, the rate has risen faster since the 1960s, yet the transition is unlikely to be complete until the start of the next century.

India has substantially more children of primary school age than any other country. On the other hand India's rapidly increasing youth will prove to be an economic asset only if they can be educated. "As the proportions of people of productive working age outnumber their dependents, there is a potential 'demographic dividend' bursting from its seams. This is a 'once

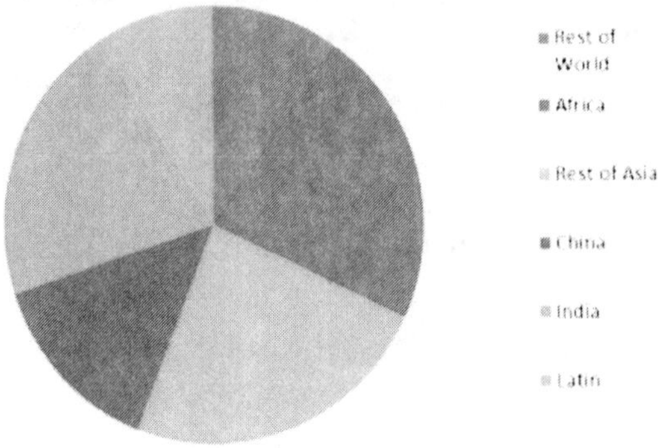

Source: (Graddol, 2010, p. 22)

Figure 4: Distribution of the world's five to nine year old children.

off' stage in a demographic transition where a rapid increase in national wealth and welfare is possible" (Graddol, 2010, p. 23).

The Social Change

Since Indians by 2010 accounted for over 17% of the global population, soon the nation will be home to over 20% of the world's productive workforce. India accounts for only 2.4 % of the world surface area and yet it supports and sustains 16.2 % of the world population. In 1950, China with 21 % share of the population was the most populous country followed by India, which had a share of 14.2 %. It is estimated that by 2050, India will overtake China to become the most populous country with about 17.2 % of global population. A rapid fall in the crude death rate (CDR) from

25.1 in 1951 to 7.6 in 2005 occurred because of technological advances and the improved quality and coverage of health care. The reduction in crude birth rate (CBR) has been less steep, declining from 40.8 in 1951 to 23.8 in 2005. (Indiastats, 2010) David Graddol predicts that, "In future, the rest of the world may look to India for workers not because they are cheap, but because that is where they can find a large pool of people with talent."(2010, p. 23)

India may have a huge population resource, but its society is ranked by interlocking divides of religion, caste, gender, age, wealth and geography. Its society is disjointed into diverse communities in a multifaceted mosaic. This fractal structure of differences and inequality, even among the poor in India, means that any social or educational innovation has different kinds and degrees of impact on its multitudes of communities and individuals. There remains always the problem, as well, that anything which promotes economic growth can also increase the gap between the rich and the poor.

Much of the oppression of the lower castes now occurs at the village level, where a variety of practices from physical intimidation to being cheated of land rights can block attempts to self-improvement.

Low caste members continue to face bias in job applications and recruitment, despite "positive discrimination" in the public sector. Sending children to English medium private schools used to be regarded as the privilege of the rich, however about developing India, Graddol writes: "McKinsey's report suggests, though, that the proportion of the population who a ling and able to pay for education is increasing fast." (2010, p.25)

Consequences of English Language Growth in India

English tends to magnify the inequality between the rich and the poor since English is rapidly becoming entrenched in the school curriculum of regional language schools, where it is often now regarded as a basic skill, necessary for employment, progression and social inclusion. Leaving access to English subject to market forces will increase the prominent class divide in common Indian society (Baldridge, 2002). Metropolitan areas are where the working middle classes grow and it is also where people from different parts of India and the world blend together inconspicuously allowing for social mobility for the lower class or caste most viable. Moreover, urban areas have always proved to be the epicentres of fashion in all spheres and aspects of life, and they have become the language acquisition centres and trend setters for English language growth and learning.

The slow process of urbanisation is a complex and contrasting phenomenon when compared with other developing and developed nations in the world. India may be urbanising faster than official statistics suggest since an increasing number of people live in districts that have developed, or been absorbed, into urban areas which are still designated as 'rural'. A town could be officially a rural town but possess all of a city's amenities such as universities, schools, hospitals, industries and a population of a few millions but it would not be in a hurry to have the district redesignated when rural status brings funding benefits from the government. This could be illustrated by the demographic statistics of the traditional city of Thanjavur in the state of Tamil Nadu in South India where according to the census data of the year of 2001, Thanjavur had a total population of 22,005,375 (Indiastats, 2010). In spite of it being classified as a rural town it had established educational institutions such as fifteen engineering colleges, four universities, a Central Research Institute teaching medical college and hospital, more than 70 Arts, Science and Education Colleges more than 120 schools and various agrobased industries. It is probable that India is following an agro-based path of development towards urbanisation. In developed countries urbanisation has been associated with depopulation of the countryside but in India it may be large towns which predominate. Historians, local literary figures, politicians and the common man of India have affirmed the view that the heart of India lies in its villages. Perhaps that is why cities tend to be regarded as a problem by politicians rather than part of the solution. Compared with China, the infrastructure in the cities of India is notoriously underdeveloped, and little attention has been given to low cost housing for workers migrating from the countryside, which could be one of the main reasons why slums proliferate in the urbanised cities of India. Even in India's cities hierarchies seem to exist as there are state government notified slums, local government notified slums, and non-notified slums existing all over the nation alongside skyscrapers and luxury hotels.

Physical Divisions Influence in India

The states of India vary on almost every measure considered so far: demographic, religious, degree of urbanisation, and perhaps most of all, sheer size. Uttar Pradesh had a population of about 197 million in 2010, whereas one of the smallest is the Himalayan state of Sikkim, with a population of 600,000. Population is increasing in all states, but the rate of growth is slowing in most. By 2026 it is expected to have started to decline in only one state, Goa, (Indiastats, 2010). India's geography ranges from the Himalayan valleys to the Great Indian Desert of Rajasthan to the backwaters of Kerala. Each of the Indian states and Union Territories has their own profile in terms of size and mix of social communities. The division between the Hindi-speaking North and the Dravidian South in India is a long-standing cultural and economic one. The populations of the southern states, which are Karnataka, Andhra Pradesh, Kerala, Tamil Nadu and Pondicherry are largely Dravidian language speakers. Their history, development record, population profiles, and economies are very different from those of the large more densely inhabited northern states, such as Madhya Pradesh, Bihar, Rajasthan and Uttar Pradesh. Kerala in the south, for example, has the highest literacy rate in India, and remittances from its many English speaking overseas citizens and middle class workers provide an important development resource. School attendance in states like Bihar in the North, meanwhile, remains stubbornly low. The eight North Eastern states form another distinct geographical zone. Connected to the rest of India by a 20km wide land corridor and all but surrounded by Nepal, Bhutan, China, Burma and Bangladesh, these states are very multilingual, but politically troubled. Several of the North Eastern states have adopted English as an official language, and many English speaking workers migrate from this area to Delhi and other urban centres where they are sought after in the services industry. (Graddol, 2010) States also differ greatly in terms of their urbanisation rates. Tamil Nadu in the South, for example, will have nearly three quarters of its populations living in urban areas by 2026, whilst Bihar in the North will not have reached 12%.

One of the big questions regarding human development in India is whether the kind of development seen today in the southern states reflects trends which will move northwards in the coming decades. One implication of states being at different stages of development is that they face very different kinds of challenges with regard to improving proficiency in English. However, the experience being acquired now in more developed areas may not be easily transferable to other parts of India because of the limitations imposed by diversity in local states.

Indian Economy

The Indian economy has been growing steadily at only a few percentage points less than China for several years. Even in the 2009–10 fiscal years, in the aftermath of a global recession, it is expected to grow around 7%. (Graddol, 2010) But, even more crucially, the economy has been expanding faster than the population, which means that the average per capita income has also been increasing, helping bring more families out of poverty, and providing more tax revenues which can support national development. Any development generates employment and since a social welfare system is nonexistent in India, employability is the driving force behind every individual in the nation. Trends in employment will have a major impact on the communication skills needed by employees. Agricultural workers have little need to communicate with people outside their communities, while services like hotels and shops will need workers who have good communication skills in relation to customers and to their own management. India's continued economic growth will depend on the availability of people who can communicate across language and cultural boundaries, both internationally and nationally (Graddol, 2010).

In India, communication skills in English are lacking not only in the large multinational companies and in the private sector but also in many public sector jobs, though it has been a pre requisite for all public sector applicants to pass intensive English language exams since the time of the ruling British Raj. Globalisation in the 21st century has eliminated many barriers to international trade, with firms pursuing global strategies to gain competitive advantage. The successful use of such strategies in this ever changing and competitive world requires new work practices exercised by a flexible workforce who are capable of engaging in transnational activities. Along with globalisation, business communication has become cross-cultural, with English being the dominant language in use. Success or failure in business relies to a great extent on the ability to communicate with flexible and fluent English. With globalisation, the importance of English as an international language in business communication has meant business people need high standards of communicative competence in both spoken and written English. Business letters involve knowledge of the rhetorical features of the genre and of the socio-cultural characteristics of the audience. As the common means of communication in global business, proficiency in English has become a core component in initiating business with international partners. It has been suggested that proficiency in the English language has become a competitive differentiator for corporate workers, companies and the entire economy, (Crystal, 2001, 2003; Graddol, 1997, 2006). Yet it remains a challenge for many non-English speaking business professionals. For over a century, English has been seen as a passport to a pensionable government job. Now, the private sector has also moved concertedly towards requiring English however more as a skill oriented requirement rather than as a theoretical and literary one.

The reasons why India appears to be following a different route are complex: poor transport infrastructure, state ownership of large enterprises, and patterns of land ownership which make it difficult to establish factories on greenfield sites, all create problems for the foreign direct investment (FDI) which plays a crucial part in a developing economy. Furthermore, there are countering forces at work during India's economic growth: such growth depends on manpower and skill becoming more productive, but after this occurs, through improved levels of training and investment in mechanisation, fewer workers are needed. Put bluntly, economic growth sends less skilled people out of work and, without improvement in education, can actually increase poverty. To compensate India is now embarking on a massive upskilling program, expanding both higher and vocational education. Government reports on Education policy have identified improving English competence as a key ingredient at all levels (Graddol, 2010).

As disposable income grows, so does the retail sector. New supermarkets, clothing shops, and malls appear. As these expand, they employ more people. The organised retail sector in India is growing, despite the problems caused by the recession. Shopping malls are opening in both metro and rural areas and are now providing new employment opportunities for school leavers and graduates with appropriate skills. Language training centres offering short term, long term, online and media supported courses are mushrooming all over the country, focussing on delivering the communication skills in English needed for employment. Courses have been tailored to cater to the market demand for those wishing to work" in malls, coffee shops or even as drivers for private cars and taxis". India still has a small tourism industry considering its size, but domestic tourists continue to outnumber international tourists by more than ten percent since the cultural diversity of India works to its advantage in tourism. It encourages locals to visit other states and territories for holidays. Because every state has its own language the linking language tends to be English and therefore workers in the hospitality trade need better communication skills in Indian languages as well as English. Tourism companies and elite hotels need English speaking drivers, who can earn 2–5 times as much as a driver elsewhere in addition to receiving the benefits of a job in the organised sector, such as health insurance and a pension (Government of India, 2003).

The IT Revolution

Business Process Outsourcing (BPO) is the process of hiring another company to handle business activities for you. BPO is distinct from information technology (IT) outsourcing, which focuses on hiring a third party company or service provider to do IT related activities, such as application management and application development, data center operations, or testing and quality assurance. In less than two decades, India's IT-BPO sector has grown from almost nothing to become a world leading industry which employs more than any other segment of the private sector economy in India. What is more, several Indian IT companies have become global operators and employ many thousands of staff in other countries. (Dossani, 2003) Many western enterprises have established their own 'captive' operations in India to provide back office and customer contact centers. Besides, it is not just the banks and technology companies that do this: the industry has had a ripple effect across Indian society.

In addition to its economic impact, it has captured the imagination of people both within and outside India and has done a great deal to 'rebrand' India as a hi- tech, forward looking country. It has also provided a model of business leadership and employment practices which has had a galvanizing impact elsewhere in the economy and in political consciousness. The sector has also opened new possibilities of social mobility, by providing well paid jobs based on merit rather than social background, but only for those who can speak English, (Graddol, 2010). The IT-BPO industry in India directly employs about 2 million people, but expects to need a further 6 million in the coming decade. It claims three times as many people are indirectly employed (Dossani, 2003). The common assumption in the education sector in India is that it just does not have the English speaking 'talent pool' to support this level of growth.

The hunt for talent is one reason why the IT-BPO revolution is spreading from the main cities into smaller towns and rural areas. A study conducted by NASSCOM and Kearney (One India, 2008) identified 50 cities which are emerging as centres for IT- BPO. Outside the metros, operational costs and salaries are lower. Tax breaks are available in the new software parks and employment zones established in development areas. But another advantage is that employees in smaller cities tend to stay there, ensuring lower attrition rates among staff. Furthermore, when a BPO starts up in a smaller city, there is often a "reverse migration" of experienced workers from the metros who are happy to find work closer to their native home towns. It is, however, more difficult to find English proficient workers in still smaller cities, and it is more difficult to maintain English as the corporate language when most workers share a common mother tongue. But the industry is keen to help local schools, colleges and "finishing schools" to develop courses which will help improve the supply of talent. The biggest impact of IT in Indian education has not been in the classroom, but in the way databases and software have created transparency in educational management. Up-to-date information about schools, staffing, pupil enrolments and dropout rates can be seen by anyone with internet access even in the subcontinent, India (Kearney, 2008).

Students, as well as public servants, have benefited from the implementation of IT in the education sector. Exam results are now widely available on the internet, and application forms for colleges, government departments and employers can be downloaded, bypassing the need to deal with officials and avoiding lengthy, often wasted, journeys. The social impact of IT has been felt in many areas of life but perhaps most of all in rural areas introduced by ITC in 2000, where IT has helped farmers by establishing internet kiosks which now reach 4 million rural families. With access to the internet, farmers can check prices of crops, get weather forecasts, find out insurance information and be informed about new developments in farming techniques (Annamalai & Rao, 2003). Around 1,000 such kiosks are alreadyoperated by local Indian entrepreneurs offering health, education and agricultural services as well as providing access to land registry with birth and death records. Such kiosks are now also offering business services with links to villages across India, and Microsoft India plans to take the opportunity to introduce 50,000 such rural kiosks. (University of California Humanities Research Institute, (UCHRI, 2010). Mobile phones have removed the long wait for landlines, and have become a key social networking tool. Their reach now extends into small towns and villages and many Indians cannot now imagine life without a cell phone. Mobile phones provide a new source of information, and are used by politicians and pressure groups to communicate with the electorate, (UCHRI, 2010).

Factories supplying low cost phones for the Indian market are now exporting to other parts of Asia and Africa, while call centres serving the domestic market are one of the fastest growing BPO sectors. A survey by the Indian market research company Juxt Consult (India Online, 2009) found that the total number of internet users in India has fallen slightly, but that the loss was mainly among casual, cyber cafe users. The survey found that around 80% of internet users are in the 19–35 age-group, mainly middle class, who typically access the internet from offices. A slowdown in internet use may signify that growth has become saturated in privileged segments of society, but that its benefits are not yet fully felt in rural areas, where mobile phones have become the main means of communication. The 2009 Indian budget, however, envisaged the rollout of broadband to 100,000 villages, and provision of internet access to rural communities is high on many corporate social responsibility (CSR) agendas. Almost all the top 100 internet sites in India, as measured by the traffic monitoring site Alexa.com, are in English, though these, like many English language websites in India, will contain some content in Hindi – in advertisements, pop up screens and comments by users. Social networking sites such as Orkut and Facebook are popular in India, especially amongst the under 25s. Orkut had an estimated 15.5 million Indian users at the end of 2009 which makes India Orkut's second largest user base globally, after Brazi), whilst Facebook had around 10.4 million A new style of low cost mobile phone, the 'chatphone ' was launched in India in 2010 (India Online, 2009).

Media

David Graddol (2010) professes that as the literacy rate in India has improved, so has the circulation of regional language newspapers. Hindi papers are, as might be expected, now the most widely read, with 41% of the total readership of dailies which is about the same proportion of Hindi speakers as there are in the population. English dailies, however, are the second most read like the '*The Times of India* 'and they have the greatest circulation. A survey of affluent families by Nielsen in 2009 has found that English is their preferred language for newspapers in India, but television is consumed more in regional languages (Rakshit, 2009). India is said to produce more films than any other country in the world and this is understandable when all the regional films are taken into account which would be more than some 1,000 movies each year. About 70% of these are in Hindi, but as they are intended to reach a national audience, and around half of the big Bollywood stars are Muslims, the language might be better described as Hindustani, with different characters speaking in ways which reflect the diversity of the film's audience.

Indian television used to be dominated by Doordarshan, the government owned and controlled state broadcaster which supplied the nation with staid national and regional programs. When private companies were licensed in 1992, commercial channels proliferated and penetrated the country's households. There are now over 300 satellite channels transmitting in India, and more than half of all households have a television since free televisions have been distributed by political parties to win popularity and votes.

Commercial channels in India need to reach the widest audience at the lowest cost and this has resulted in a focus on a few languages. The main beneficiary language in this massive media revolution, however, is not English. Since Hindi and the local language of every region and state reach a substantially larger audience for general entertainment, the channel operators and media companies have the greatest returns: Hindi entertainment is thought to account for 55% of advertising revenue and so can justify high levels of investment in production values. Rupert Murdoch, owner of Star TV, said as early as 1994, "The notion under democracy is that a TV franchise must allow independent editorial and creative judgment within it" (Observer Review, 2003).

Currently, most English films, documentaries, dramas and even children's animated shows like Disney productions, are often dubbed into Hindi or the local regional language of every region and state for broadcasting and advertisement purposes. The dominance of Indian languages extends also to children's television, since the common people of India tend to consider English as the language of business. Information and news through the electronic media at their door step from around the world is preferred in the local language as it is the preferred language for entertainment too. Nevertheless for a large proportion of patriotic Indian parents their media is not local enough, with an absence of locally made culturally influencing programming and too much dubbing of Western made popular soaps and documentaries. In a large percentage of households children are now learning the local language rather than English, from television. The dominance of the local language may decline slightly as the media market grows, as has been seen with the evolution of the global internet; it was first dominated by English, but developed into a multilingual space as it matured. Similarly, television may diversify linguistically, as the consumer market in India grows and companies attempt to reach into minority market segments.

Education System in India

Every village and city street in the developing states of India has a public school claiming to impart education to children through English medium, although knowledge of English language in the faculty of these street schools is very feeble and they quietly resort to Hindi medium or to the state's language medium of education. Nonetheless, to attract parents of school age children, they prominently display English medium on the facades and signage of their buildings. Apart from these street schools, every town and city has a good number of English medium public schools with palatial buildings to attract the parents eager for English education for their kids. Just for having nice buildings, such public schools charge the parents tuition fees ranging from 10 to 50 times that charged by street public schools. Several state governments have bowed to public pressure and introduced English medium streams in their schools. This may not be the best approach for children. In the minds of many parents, it seems that English-medium education is the best. This seems to be the reason for both the growth of private schooling and the increased shift towards English as a medium of instruction in some government schools (Graddol, 2010). In the majority of these schools, the family environments are mother tongue oriented; without the reinforcement of English at home and children fail to grasp crucial elements of the knowledge taught them at school through the English medium. Both the parents and the teachers understand this but, for various reasons, insist on attempting to educate children using English medium. Parents believe that English language based learning is the pathway to high achievement. Teachers insist on English-medium education to persuade the public that they are producing the elite class in the country. Apart from hefty tuition fees, another great source of income to public schools are the purchase of books by students as the costlier the book, higher the commission for the school. Consequently, schools tend to prescribe books to children which are heavier in weight and costlier in price, without even seeing whether the contents are appropriate to their targeted students. Of course, parents are apt to feel proud that their children are studying very heavy and costly books, but the reality is that the children may be deriving little benefit from them.

Teachers know quite well that their students are incapable of fully comprehending lessons from their prescribed texts, so they don't rely on teaching the students but simply guide the students to tick mark some words and phrases in the books and cram those in order to achieve a passing grade in their examinations. In these schools the percentage of secured marks by the students is kept unusually high, in the range from 70 to 90, making the parents more proud of their children after seeing their secured marks. English medium schools have obtained much of their academic reputation from the fact that parents who were wealthy enough to pay the fees were themselves well educated, and often English speaking at home. Some private schools today maintain their exclusivity by using the educational level of parents as an admission criterion and insisting on a 'donation', which only the wealthiest can afford. The top ranking private schools are well-resourced and employ well trained and experienced teachers. However, English medium teaching is no magic solution; without both quality teachers and apt students' English medium teaching by itself yields small benefit and Graddol (2010) affirms with the view that "The result is a child who has neither English nor much education and the social divide is increased."

According to government figures, (Indiastats, 2010) enrolment in English medium schools at upper primary is at an all-time high, having increased a sharp *74 percent in just three years* during 2003-2006. The most dramatic increases are in the southern states:

Andhra Pradesh	- 100 percent increase (from 10.6 lakh to 20.9 lakh)
Tamil Nadu	- 17 percent increase (from 14.7 lakh to 17.2 lakh)
Maharashtra	- 12 percent increase (10.6 lakh to 11.9 lakh)
Punjab (up by 93 ,000) and Himachal Pradesh	- both 4 percent increase each
Karnataka	- 2 percent increase
Kerala	- 3 percent increase (from 2.4 lakh to 3.2 lakh)

It is clearly worth asking the question: what are the significant reasons behind such a widespread Indian preference for educating children in English medium schools.

The most commonly answered, discussed and recorded opinions by researchers are:

1. People feel that only English can help their kids do well in life because higher education in India is in English and all employers prefer people who speak English
2. Some places have a larger number of good quality English medium schools than vernacular medium schools and parents want the best school for their children.
3. There is a loss of faith in government schools, most of which are not English medium schools.
4. A large number of Indians in urban areas see English as a good link language in a country where many languages are spoken. They also see English as a global link language.A large number of Indians think that English has become an Indian language and in fact we have developed our own version of English. They do not think of it as an alien language.

5. English carries with it some element of "snob value" and everyone wants to learn it to increase their social status.

As India reinvents itself in a new era of globalised economy and social mobility, linguistic diversity will prove to be an important resource both economically and, through multilingual development, for national integration. Providing education for all children in their mother tongue is a problem in many states. Sometimes a de facto 'four language formula' is used, in which children are taught in their first language, but also have to learn the regional language, Hindi and English. In other cases, children are unable to attend a school that teaches in their mother tongue, and they start their educational career in a language which may not be used at home. Although all children in India are supposed to receive basic education in their mother tongue, it is clear that most people in non Hindi speaking states grow up learning 2 Indian languages plus English and often take up a foreign language as well. As they enter college, English is the medium of instruction and although Hindi is not compulsory anymore, a language other than English is compulsory for humanities courses. Students who feel disinclined to start learning a new language like French, often take Hindi, as they are already proficient at it after having learnt it at school. And in any case, not all colleges offer the students the facilities needed for learning a foreign language like French or German. French and German are the most popular foreign languages, although this is changing and students are showing a lot of interest in Chinese and Japanese. Hindi is now heard in some domains, such as consumer advertising, which used to be predominantly English. However, the reverse trend is also true, the proportion of English in Hindi and local language film dialogues, for example, has increased. Code switching between English and Hindi, popularly known as 'Hinglish', 'Tinglish' among Tamil language speakers, and 'Kinglish' among Kanada language speakers, now features in the speech of many Indians.

Problems

Regional languages issue still provide a platform for political activists in several states. Regional language politics are sometimes aimed at Hindi, sometimes at English, and sometimes at migrant or minority communities. India is home to many languages, and its constitution, education system and working practices recognise this. Education systems tend to value only some languages and may attempt to eradicate the variety and fluidity in language use that children bring to school. This is one of the ways in which education encourages language loss. English is in greater demand in India than ever before as parents and employers want it, and public policy increasingly accepts the need to provide universal access to it. On the other hand, how can opportunities for learning English be provided efficiently and effectively in such a diverse and dynamic environment. In response to a rising demand from parents for English medium education today, education authorities across India are introducing more English into government schools. Arguments about the medium of schooling have run for many years, often spilling into the law courts. The belief and trend that an English education leads to higher education and better jobs is predominantly true, and it is seen by lower castes as an escape route from social imprisonment. Across the cross section of India, English medium education is believed to work to disperse educational outcomes. For a small minority, it results in better English skills but no better general educational outcomes. This small minority, who have an "English friendly" environment, an English -94- medium education poses no hurdle, or a very small one. But the rewards are linked to opportunities in the global marketplace for higher education and jobs, including the export oriented service industries in India. However, for the large majority, English medium education works differently, leading to poorer educational outcomes and poorer language skills, and this is a matter of great concern to education administrators.

This divide between 'private' English medium schools and 'public' Government regional language schools, has historically reflected the divide between English medium and vernacular medium schools. In other words, an elite minority learns through English medium in school, is better prepared for the challenge of university courses taught through English, and provides the main source of students on postgraduate degrees, such as the MBA, MCA., M.Phil., Ph.D., etc. which lead to the best paid careers. Indian education now appears to be on the same track as most of the rest of the world in integrating English into the curriculum as a basic skill for all children.

Graddol (2010) in his book '*English Next India*' identifies seven scenarios through which proficiency in English is developed in Indians. The role and importance of each varies according to the age and career point of the learner, but all play a role in creating English speakers in India. These scenarios can be confirmed from Graddol's qualitative and quantitative research statistics. The first ideal circumstance for English language development has to be the home and community. Children who come from homes where English is spoken by parents or even a domestic helper, gain a head start in English, and also are supported in schoolwork.

Communities such as the English speaking Anglo Indians or the Christians, offer considerably more exposure to English to children out of school. Secondly, the years of compulsory education at primary school level now provide a new focus for English teaching, though practice and quality varies greatly. Whichever language skills are thought necessary as part of a child's general education, even if it is for someone who does not pursue an academic route, they need to be acquired by the age of 14, underlining the importance of learning the English language at primary school. Thirdly, the secondary schools teach students in the age group between fifteen to eighteen and have traditionally focused on teaching English as a subject, and in concurrently teaching subjects through English medium in the private schools. Neither approach is very effective in developing skills in using the language efficiently. Fourthly, it is clear that many parents and learners rely on private supplementation for English learning, such as private language institutes, coaching colleges, private tuition and other provisional caters for all age groups, but access to these facilities are better in urban areas and service the richer families. Subsequently, universities and colleges have in the past decade become more concerned and aware about the 'employability' of their graduates and many now offer co-curricular courses in English communication skills.

Consequently, many employers help make up for the skills gap by in house training and using other avenues like, workplace and corporate training. Finally, informal learning for many Indians plays an important 'finishing role' in moulding and shaping them and giving them credentials to survive in the fast paced, competitive environment that they need to succeed and survive in . Individuals who study overseas especially in English speaking nations come back with improved English skills. Opportunities for overseas study have tended to be available more for richer, middle class families, but the increased availability of student loans and scholarships, and the fact of innumerable overseas universities opening tempting and viable opportunities, has seen an exodus of Indian students to the world.

Since India attained Independence on 15th August 1947, the focus in Indian education has been on increasing the number of children attending schools and providing basic facilities and amenities such as new schools and classrooms, drinking water, toilets and infrastructure. However, the government schools in India continue to be much less well equipped than those of other developing nations in the 21st century, such as their counterparts in China. The poor performance of children in the majority of Indian government primary schools has manifold causes, some relating to the teachers and their training, a few to the institutional contexts in which they work, some to the methodologies and textbooks being used, and yet others to the social background and family circumstances of the students themselves. This has made it extremely difficult to identify any single intervention which might remedy the situation. It also means that improvement at primary level will take much longer than is needed to meet the dual aspirations to improve access to secondary and higher education whilst improving the quality of learning outcomes at each stage (Graddol, 2010). The situation seems scarcely better in secondary schools. The track record of secondary schools in developing written English skills is dismal, but now the priority is for speaking skills, and to start the business of English teaching in primary schools. This will require well trained and qualified teachers, using communicative methods to engage young learners; however, introducing the teaching of English into schools where trained teachers and suitable textbooks do not exist will produce only educational failure.

Apart from in those states which have adopted English as their official language, the general pattern in India has long been for children in government schools to be taught in a regional language, and for children in private schools to be taught through English. Only a small percentage of the Indian population belongs to an elite layer of society which is able to negotiate each stage of the education system with relative ease. Of this small percentage, many speak English to some extent before they enter primary school, or come from homes in which English is spoken. They hear people speaking in English every day. They see their parents reading a daily newspaper in English. They attend a well-equipped English medium school staffed by well qualified teachers. The term 'convent school' is often used as a generic term for the best English medium private schools, indicating their origin as a place that sought to provide students not only with high levels of scholarship, but also values. Students from such schools provide a high flying intake to universities, especially institutions such as IIMs and IITs. Unfortunately, these institutions do not fully apply the reservation quotas that could overcome disparity and help bring the underprivileged castes closer to enjoying the opportunities that belong to the privileged elite upper caste in the Indian social order.

In most states, primary education is provided in regional and minority languages, in addition to English as a second language, and private schools at all levels provide English medium education. The principle being followed is that most children in public government funded schools begin their education in their mother tongue with English being taught as a second language while at private educational institutions the reverse occurs.

In the case of minority language children, such as those who speak tribal languages, more is now being done to support mother tongue learning in early years, but it is typically seen as a transitional arrangement, preparing children for study in the regional language as soon as possible. At each stage in the education system, the three language formula expects that a language other than the current medium of education will be taught as a subject, often as a preparation towards shifting to study through that language at the next educational level. Secondary education is often associated with a move up the language hierarchy, with most schools teaching either through the regional language, Hindi or English. On the other hand, according to Graddol's research statistics for "English Next India" (2010, p83), "only around 60% of the age groups reach this stage, and there is significant drop out during the secondary years, with only 28% of students reaching Class 11–12. At college and university, the proportion of courses taught through English is very much higher, though the participation rate in higher education is only around 12%." Nevertheless, a broad consensus seems now to be developing that the goal of Indian education should be to create multilingual speakers.

The private sector has always played an important role in Indian education, but in recent years, since the middle and developing class has evolved in the subcontinent, there has been a continuous, momentous increase in parents sending their children to private schools. More parents across India, both the rich and poor, are sending or aiming to send their children to private schools. Even in rural areas more children now attend private primary schools, and more boys than girls are likely to attend reflecting the gender bias in existence across the nation. The boost in enrolments in the private education sector ultimately reflects every Indian parent's desire for English medium education. Teachers in government schools are paid higher remuneration, often have higher educational qualifications and are better trained than their counterparts in many private schools. But students nevertheless seem to learn better in private schools and consistently the end results are better. These contrasting results may result to different relationships that exist between parent and school in the private system. The private schools and their teachers depend on maintaining a good customer focused relationship with the parent. If parents feel that their child is unhappy, or is not learning, they will withdraw their child. This relationship may be closer in rural and slum areas, where many unrecognised private schools are small, single room affairs and teachers often live in the same area. Children, especially in the primary classes, are given a lot more attention in private schools. Teachers in government schools who offer private tuition out of school may not go out of their way to ensure the children learn in class and to make matters worse the teachers in government schools are typically of a higher caste than the children they teach and, involuntarily (for such behaviour is prohibited), this social relationship is re-enacted in the government classroom: lower caste children are more often beaten, slandered and less often praised. Higher caste children often bully classmates of a lower caste and segregate them. Such discriminatory behaviour is not sufficiently exposed and criticised since it is the way of life in the day to day, social and communal life in India.

More children in India are being taught through English, not just because of the rise of private schools but because English is introduced in government schools. State and central governments are trying to respond to the competition from the private sector by starting new government schools in English medium and by also introducing English medium streams in the regular government run regional language schools. In Tamil Nadu, some primary schools have had to be closed due to lack of student enrolments because of a combination of falling birth rates and a drift towards private English medium schools. In many states, even where English medium education is not adopted, English is now being introduced into the curriculum of government schools from Class 1. With the growing use of English medium education, more schools are abandoning regional exam boards and affiliating to central government run education boards, named either as the Central Board of Secondary Education (CBSE) or the Indian School Certificate Exam (ISCE). These boards have greater prestige and offer a nationally understood standard which is often sought after by parents who desire English medium education for their children. CBSE also implements the (NCERT) curriculum recommendations closely, and is the first to reflect changes in central government policy. The English syllabus of the CBSE is considered to be more manageable than that of ICSE because it offers a broad based syllabus which is generally perceived to be sound, in spite of issues that need to be debated in the current scenario of focused approach to curriculum. However, it increases the load on students, thus leading to stress in spite of the student being given the option of studying only the basic languages of his or her choice, which could be English or another regional language. CBSE has in recent years been very proactive in devising new courses that are academic with a vocational slant. It has become more responsive to the needs of a dynamically changing pedagogical scenario. A concept of "Front Line Curriculum" has been put in place in CBSE that requires syllabi be studied on an ongoing basis and 10 per cent of irrelevant or out dated material is replaced with more pertinent matter, however it incorporates no academically designed process or program for syllabi revision and upgrading.

The number of students who leave school with English medium qualifications which have a national currency is increasing, and this is likely to help the mobility of students across state boundaries, especially since the school leaving higher secondary exams of class 12 have come to be used as the main entrance qualification for universities. One remaining constraint on mobility is that university candidates often lose their eligibility for a reservation quota, which again is solely based on their caste ethnicity, outside their own state. This may change if the "unique identification card" project is successfully implemented by the central government. A quarter of children in early primary schools are now first generation learners who subsequently have little support from the family and community, and must rely for their learning on what happens in school (Graddol, 2010). Nevertheless where first generation learners do attend English medium schools, the sacrifices made by their family to make this possible create an additional stress for them. It may also be difficult for the child to deal with the different worlds of home and school. First generation learners often have to act as family 'interpreters', helping their parents understand notices or letters that contain English, or acting as a go between with school officials, teachers and the external world.

Many of the challenges faced by the first generation learner of English are wider one fecting access to education by lower caste children. Children in village schools are less likely to hear English being spoken, or see it on signs or advertising. Even in towns, English is more prevalent on the main roads than in the side streets, both in written and spoken form. In the rural areas, away from the highways, English is less used, seen or heard, and some schools counter this by introducing more English into the school environment. For example, English notices may be displayed prominently, and English will be used in assemblies and in classroom teaching and discussion. Some schools are successfully using English audio materials, such as the 'interactive radio' lessons. One benefit of such schemes is that teachers learn alongside the pupils. Success is due not just to the quality of their teachers, but also due to the support from the learners' families, including other siblings and parents, and community outreach programs. Progress among the cohort of first generation learners has always proven to be slow, however by the second generation the pace picks up as more children in the class have parents who speak, or at least understand, English. Furthermore, their teachers will subsequently have better English language communication skills and evidently that could lead to more English being spoken, learnt and gained in the learning scenario.

The introduction of English teaching in early primary schools in India reflects wider trends in English education around the world. Universities in many countries began to require students of any subject to reach a certain standard of English proficiency before they could obtain their degree. In theory the proficiency level to be achieved was IELTS 6.0, but in practice, given the poor starting levels and, at times, indifferent motivation of students, rarely exceeded FCE/IELTS 5.5, (Graddol, 2010). This level is not regarded as sufficient for academic study through the medium of English, or for professional use. However, a minimum proficiency level in English is increasingly regarded as an entrance requirement for university. This is now the norm in most western education providers and universities in the United Kingdom, United State, Canada and Australia to name a few. Even where university teaching is not conducted through English, students may be expected to be able to understand English textbooks. The growing role of English in higher education is one reason why a new global orthodoxy has emerged with primary learning beginning at primary school, where they learn the basics of the language, then develop English as a language of study into secondary school. Another reason for embedding English in the basic curriculum is that it has become a global lingua franca which will be useful for all students, especially those who get jobs in the services sector. For this reason, some countries now expect all school leavers to attain a level equivalent to at least B1 which is on the Common European Framework of Reference for Languages (CEFR) and equivalent to:

TOEFL	233	(computer-based)
TOEFL	90	(internet-based)
IELTS:		Competent User, Band 6.0 (Little, 2011)

Achieving this level of proficiency in India will be a challenge, since compulsory schooling is completed by age fourteen. There is, however, a need to decide on a minimum level of English as one of the expected outcomes of universal education. In teaching English to young learners it is essential to consider how children learn. There are recognised stages of cognitive development that every child passes through, and teaching material should take account of this. There is also a great need for the motivation to learn English for both the pupils and the teachers. The majority of primary school teachers have an insufficient command of English to be able to teach it effectively. Teachers with insufficient subject knowledge have very little, if any, confidence. Without subject knowledge, subject application cannot take place, and it is unfair to place expectations on primary school teachers of child centred learning or of related participatory practices. Where should they start if they do not understand the materials and their own knowledge of the language is uncertain? Lack of subject knowledge is one of the main causes of the present problems in teaching English in primary schools. The teachers are not assisted by their materials. The materials are not prepared with the level of available teacher expertise in mind. The teachers need help and it is not being provided. Not even minimum training is being afforded to teachers when what they require is concerted and intensive training.

The goal of the education sector in India is to lay down minimum levels of learning (MLL) irrespective of caste, creed, location or sex, so that all children are given access to education of a comparable standard. This can be achieved if Graddols ' (2010) recommended model of English teaching is adopted and implemented. Firstly, an awareness for the necessity, benefits and importance of learning the language needs to be developed across the nation as a whole. Secondly, English as a subject has to become a part of all existing school curriculums with the focus on communicative language acquisition using written texts, vocabulary and grammar. The teaching methods need to be varied: students reading aloud from the book in turn, or in chorus; students consistently working by writing on the blackboard; students not only copying from the board or textbook but acquiring comprehension skills in reading and writing guided by questioning and answering.

Finally, teachers need to be trained to teach through English and not through translation. Special language support would have to be provided where required for students and teachers so that students can effectively acquire English language skills. When a subject is simply taught through English, little learning is believed to take place as the subject's comprehension could be in the mother tongue and memorisation could easily be achieved. However when the focus is on teaching communicative language skills, practice of these skills forms a key component of teaching.

Language is acquired automatically in the process of communication and learning. This methodology and the efficiency of it seem to be making it the most popular method at present at both ends of the educational spectrum, from the young primary learner to the "finishing" classes in institutes and universities.

India does not have adequate English proficient teachers to implement the programs now being instigated on a national basis. This is a common obstacle faced by most developing countries in the world which seek to provide English to their children, nevertheless in India the scale of the problem is greater. Affluent countries like Saudi Arabia or the United Arab Emirates regard it as essential to import "native speakers" of English as teachers to supplement local teachers and train them, however this approach tends to cause as many problems as it solves. India has long been a net exporter of English teachers, supplying schools and universities elsewhere in the world, including Singapore and the Middle East and Africa. Some Asian countries have, in recent years, accepted that Indian teachers can be regarded as 'native speakers' of English. The current Eleventh Five-Year Plan (Government of India, 2007) has aspired to universally introduce English in primary school at least from Class 3 onwards. In reality, several states have gone further and are now attempting to introduce English from Class 1 onwards.

It is doubtful that teachers at lower primary level will be able to do this successfully with the limited skills, facilities and training available to them. The standard of English among teachers often reflects their own level of education and tends to be particularly poor among older teachers in lower primary schools since most of them have not had any professional development to keep pace with evolving new methodologies in teaching, especially those which utilise new technology.

The British Council was asked by the Tamil Nadu government to test the speaking skills of a group of upper primary teachers prior to a training program in 2009. The teachers were required to have a BA or equivalent in English and to have undergone earlier training, so the group cannot be regarded as representing the general range of teachers. Most of the group reached the B1 threshold, but few reached C1 (Graddol, 2010). If this is the situation among teachers who have received training the common truth existing among the English teachers is undeniably very low and it is an area of concern that cannot be solved easily because of the many factors, social and political that comes into play.

The Higher Education System in India

The higher education system in India has grown in a remarkable way, particularly in the post independence period, to become one of the largest systems of its kind in the world. However, the system faces many difficulties at present: financing and management concerns, including access, equity and relevance; a needed reorientation of programs, laying emphasis on health consciousness, values and ethics; a need to establish quality standards of higher education by reviewing the assessment of institutions and their accreditation. These issues are important for the country, as it is now engaged in the use of higher education as a powerful tool to build a knowledge based information society of the 21st century. Universities have to perform multiple roles, creating new knowledge, acquiring new capabilities and producing an intelligent human resource pool; they must accomplish this through challenging teaching, research and extension activities so as to balance both the need and the demand. Recognizing and achieving these goals is a very high undertaking for the planners and implementers of education policy in India.

The Indian higher education system has undergone massive expansion in post independent India with a national resolve to establish several universities, technical institutes, research institutions and professional and non-professional colleges all over the country. The goal is to generate and disseminate knowledge coupled with the noble intention of providing easy access to higher education for the common Indian. Public initiatives played a dominant and controlling role in this phase. Most of the universities were public institutions with powers to regulate academic activities on their campuses, as well as in their areas of jurisdiction through the affiliating system. Even the private institutions enjoyed large scale financial support in the form of grants from the public exchequer. Private funds as well as individuals played key roles in the cause of higher education. With public funding no longer being adequate for the challenging task of expansion and diversification of the higher education system in the country, with its many continuously growing demands, there has been little option than to bring in private initiatives in a massive way. The deregulating mechanism of controls started with the granting of "Autonomous Status" to identified colleges in the 1970s. Some of these colleges have graduated further to receive the "Deemed to be University" status in later years. (University Grants Commission [UGC], 2003).

Quick access to information has made knowledge creation fast, and the multiplier effect has made it even explosive. It is increasingly difficult to anticipate changes and respond to them with creative purpose. Designing courses with relevance to the future and developing the necessary manpower to deliver them is a challenging task for the higher education system in India since it is a hierarchical one in terms of prestige. At the apex are "Institutions of National Importance" (INIs), including the IIScs, IITs, IIMs, and NITs. These are intended to be globally competitive institutions. There were 13 such institutions in 2006, but the number had expanded to around 50 by 2009. Below these INIs are the Central Universities which were around 30 in 2009, and below that the State Universities which again are around 250. The present archaic administrative practices need a thorough reform (UGC, 2003), for a healthy public/private partnership can do much in this regard by way of exchanging good practices. A management system, lean but professional, making use of modern communication and information technologies, is required to facilitate quality higher education.

According autonomous status to all performing institutions will facilitate rapid development of efficient and state of the art higher education institutions. However, the policies are not fully implemented mostly because of faulty management of the institutions of higher education. The administrative structure of the universities, which was devised in the pre independence period, seems to be continuing. The new challenges facing the system of higher education in the country cannot be met without a total overhaul of the structure of management of higher education institutions. This has become all the more necessary because of globalization, which requires talent, competence, drive, initiative and innovation at several levels. This cannot be achieved without overhauling the administrative set up of universities and higher education institutions generally. Because of the growing interdependence and integration of the world economy in recent years, the Indian higher education system has a new role and a challenge to provide to the nation and the world at large, skilled human resources at all levels, having breadth of knowledge and confidence to effectively confront the social and economic realities.

It is worth noting that while India boasts a vast system of higher education, second only to that of the USA, the total number of students hardly represent 6 percent of the relevant age group, i.e., 18 - 23, which is much below the average of developed countries, which is about 47%. Thus, access, equity, accountability and quality should form the four guiding principles in the planning of higher education development in India in the 21st century. It is true that enhancing social access to higher education is important in rural areas but the major challenge before the Indian higher education system is to bring equity in quality of education across the length and breadth of the country. The goal close to the heart of students everywhere, whether it be in rural, semi urban and urban areas is to be able to participate in the new economic revolution.

A number of social, economic and political factors seem to act as constraints to access equity in higher education in India. Poverty leads to high dropout rates even at primary, middle and secondary school levels. The lower status of women, lack of easy access, lack of implementation of existing programs, inadequate utilization of resources, absence of political will, and inadequacies in coordinated actions across all equity fronts within institutions, also seem to be factors. Financial constraints also often form a significant factor in delaying the achievement of equity (UGC, 2003), however the vast majority of graduates in India study in one of the many thousands of "affiliated colleges", an increasing number of which are private institutions of which there are over 75% engineering and medical colleges, and 66% of management and teacher training colleges. (University Grants Commission (2003). Since student enrolment in these disciplines has recently surged, this represents a significant growth of the private sector in higher education. Students in these colleges sit for exams set by the universities.

The system of affiliation, established by the British on the then model of London University, is regarded as one of the main obstacles to achieving excellence. Less than 2% of higher education institutions award their own degrees. Indian universities barely register in world rankings of academic quality: only two appear in the *Times Higher Education* top 200, while, curiously, a different two Indian universities appear in the 'Top 500' world ranking published by Shanghai Jiao Tong University, China (The Times, 2010). Restrictions on foreign universities operating in India are in the process of being relaxed and several are already planning to open facilities or joint programs. Imperial College, London, which helped set up IIT-Delhi in the 1960s, is one of the highest ranking world universities, and it may be one of the first prestigious universities to start operating a campus in the subcontinent. (Graddol, 2010) The globalisation of knowledge, and of higher education itself, is contributing to an increasing use of English as the medium of education.

Students seeking to study in an English speaking country are required to have a proficiency level in English of at least C1 on the CEFR and this equates to about B and 6.5 of the IELTS test, which as commonly known is one of the most popular tests taken by international students. The C1 level is also regarded as the minimum required for professional employment in any business which uses English as its working language. There is no data on the English proficiency levels of students in Indian universities and colleges. Vice-chancellors and professors, however, even in top tier education institutions, talk of a large skills gap, even at postgraduate level, between the actual level of students and that expected by employers and this suggests a level well below C1.

English in Vocational Education

For centuries, Indian crafts people and artisans have created great architecture and art. But these people acquired their skills mainly informally, and children today are still often born into their future occupations. This has made it difficult to expand skilled trades quickly in India and to regulate them in the ways required by modernity. Vocational education has long been neglected in a world in which academic study is more highly valued. Vocational educational in India aims to develop skilled manpower through diversified courses to meet the requirements of mainly the unorganised sector and to teach self-employment skills to people through a large number of self-employment oriented courses. One of the weaknesses of the Indian education system is that it does not give due importance to vocational education. As a result there is a mismatch between the skilled manpower required and skilled manpower available.

Given the rate at which the economy and the youth population of the country is burgeoning, if the current shortfall is not met in terms of developing a more skilled workforce, we run the risk of high unemployment which would, in turn, adversely impact the fortunes of the country. The current size of vocational education is estimated at US$ 1.4 billion and is expected to grow to US$ 5.8 billion, a CAGR of 15.3 percent. It is estimated that 90 million jobs will be created over the next five years, of which almost half (45 million) are expected in the services sector. Of these, an estimated 7-10 million are expected to be created in hospitality, healthcare, and modern retail alone. (Jasuja, 2007) Of these new jobs, more than half would require some form of vocational training. At present, many businesses feel they have to remedy deficiencies in the education system through in house training, and they resent this additional cost. Employers in all countries tend to complain about the poor literacy and communication skills of school leavers and graduates, however, it is not always clear where responsibility should lie.

The role of public education is not just to train for jobs, but to create citizens with skills that can be adapted to many career eventualities, and to enable them fully to exercise their rights and responsibilities, including in their roles as consumers in a democratic society. Larger Indian businesses are already partnering with government departments to help improve the English and employability skills of both students in colleges and those in vocational education. Many large companies have similar relationships with local colleges, helping ensure that students acquire sound communication skills before they graduate. A problem faced by any general purpose "English for the workplace" training course is that job related skills are often specific to context. Each work domain has its own special requirements with regard to communication and there may be particular kind of reports or forms to be filled in or perhaps interactions with customers that need to conform to a corporate policy. For these reasons, workplace English training is best carried out using materials taken from the workplace itself. In India the main focus seems now to be on the concept "English for employability".

Graddol (2010) in his *English Next India* affirms, with the backing of substantial research, that the "equal importance of English skills in career progression is the glass ceiling for non-English speakers". Role profiling allows employers to identify the minimum level of skill required to carry out a particular job function. Profiling helps recruiters select candidates, but can also be used to audit the skills of existing employees and so identify areas requiring further training. Another value of profiling is that it can clarify and make explicit the competencies actually needed in particular job roles, given that what an employer imagines is needed is not always what an employee finds most crucial in everyday work. According to government plans, of the 15 million students who need vocational education every year, about 5 million students would be provided initial training by strengthening existing VET institutions and by setting up new ones. The remaining 10 million students would be trained through non formal and informal modes. The Government also plans to encourage the participation of the private sector and NGOs in a number of areas: in improvement of the facilities and resources of VET institutions, in development of skills and skill standards, of training packages, of competency based curricula and of instructional materials in conducting tests, and in providing joint certification (Jasuja, 2007).

However, there are two dimensions to the "talent pool" crisis in India: firstly, there is the question whether the education system is producing a sufficient number of graduates to satisfy the demand; secondly, is the quality of the graduates the system does produce good enough to meet the skill requirements? Much of the "talent pool" crisis in India at present relates to the number of graduates who apparently lack "employability skills". The Information Technology Business Process Outsourcing (IT-BPO) industry organisation constantly complains about the "low employability of existing talent with only 10–15% employable graduates in business services and 26% employable engineers in technology services". This perceived shortfall needs to be put into perspective. Employers in most countries have complained about "falling standards", or a "skills gap", ever since national education systems were invented (Thomex.com, 2011). There are at least two reasons for such continued skills shortages. Primarily, any fast-moving and expanding economy needs an ever more skilled workforce, year on year, and, in such circumstances, education systems are bound to struggle to upgrade the level of their students fast enough. Next, graduate employability is not just a symptom of a failing education system but a reflection of an ongoing debate in all countries about the role of universities and schools, and the respective merits of training versus education (Graddol,2010).

Should schools and universities be training people for specific jobs, or equipping their students with skills which will have a broader and longer term value? Employability skills fall uneasily between these two categories. The debate about "employability skills" in India also reflects the gap between expected social behaviour in a modern, urban society and perceived norms amongst the uneducated, rural classes. Many of the "soft skills" sought after by employers are thus not especially related to the English language, but do relate to the kind of interpersonal skills that more school leavers and graduates will need as the services sector expands. IT-BPO companies have specific requirements for these skills to be delivered through English, but if the domestic economy including the "Business Process Outsourcing" sector continues to grow as expected, workers will in future need these skills in other Indian languages. In particular, the ability to switch between languages in order to carry out customer facing duties in one language and internal administrative work like dealing with managers, reading instructions and briefings, filling in forms, and attending meetings in another sphere, will be increasingly in demand.

The traditional allocation of English to the workplace and regional language to the private sphere is in process of changing, and has begun to change at a fast pace in major metropolitan cities. Many of the better universities now provide co-curricular courses in English communication and in soft skills to ensure that their graduates are employable. The larger employers are also working closely with the universities and colleges which supply their new recruits. But many colleges do not provide such courses, or do not have the qualified staff to do so. This forces students into the private sector finishing schools to bridge the gap between skill and qualification. Many employers, however, now follow the maxim that you must "hire the attitude, and train the skills" (Graddol 2010). In other word hire people of the right character traits and habits, which cannot easily be established by short term training, and then add the skills that short term training can provide quite effectively. Sound character traits, of course, may reflect early education. For example, it is difficult to imagine that children now following the activity based learning schemes introduced in Tamil Nadu schools will not be independent and confident learners later in life. Ability and willingness to learn are now two of the most sought after skills among recruiters in India.

Some of the challenges relating to English in Indian education are shared by other countries at a similar stage of economic and social development. Others are probably unique to India. Improving education is seen as a key ingredient in human and economic development, enabling millions to escape from poverty. This is generally followed by a slowing of population growth and an improvement in the health and social welfare of ordinary people. Achieving such goals requires a huge investment in education at all levels, and a shortage of resources is a common problem. In India, however, this is not now the main problem. The problem of corruption especially plagues projects relating to infrastructure development, procurement and recruitment. Highly bureaucratic procedures designed to control corruption in government departments make it difficult for corrupt employees to redirect funds and equipment, unfortunately have the effect of hindering innovation and preventing employment for more people. Such procedures make it difficult to ensure projects are effectively and quickly delivered and bureaucratic complexity also reduces transparency and accountability to external stakeholders. A shortage in the workforce available for managing and delivering large scale public sector projects, from policy to local actuality, is an even larger problem. Huge projects in terms of the numbers of children and teachers affected are characteristically managed by surprisingly small teams. There is a lack of trained and experienced project managers, of people who can monitor and supervise projects, and of trainers at all levels (Graddol 2010).

These limitations make it very difficult to scale up successful pilot projects to a point where they have significant social and economic impact. In a country like India, where much of the electorate is poorly educated or illiterate, it is difficult to achieve a well informed public debate about language choice in education. At worst, such a debate could even reduce the political will for genuine educational progress amongst the masses because the size of the investment needed would be difficult for politicians to promote. India is arguably the fastest developing nation in the world and the fight over mass education is about changing the political culture of the largest, but also one of the most corrupted, democracies in the world. Electorates who are educated and well informed need to be persuaded in different ways from those who are under educated.

In India, access to English provides access to the national political debate. Language politics in developing countries add further to the difficulty of introducing effective educational reform. There are significant regional tensions and loyalties surrounding languages, often related to tribal or other social, religious and ethnic divisions. Many developing countries are former colonies, in which a European language is added to the mix, often as a language of privilege. In former colonies which were not British both English and the former colonial language typically fight for position in educational policies. (Graddol 2010). In multilingual countries like Sri Lanka, Malaysia or Singapore language policy is nearly always a dispute over power and identity, not just a question about which forms of education are most effective from a monetary or pedagogic point of view. Decisions about the medium of instruction, and which languages are taught, provide an important gate keeping mechanism that determines who gains admission into the best jobs and to future cultural, economic and political power.

Issues

Efficient teacher supply is another recurrent problem in developing countries, especially where the population is growing rapidly. The pool of educated adults is small in comparison to the large numbers of children who need to be taught. English teachers tend to be in especially short supply. Anyone who can speak English can usually find a much better paid job elsewhere in the economy, making both recruitment and retention of English teachers difficult, particularly in rural areas. Currently employed English teachers who have spent their careers teaching grammar and literature may not have the skills to teach spoken English, at this moment regarded as the starting point for most English curriculums. Increasing the amount of English in the curriculum is typically a part of wider educational reforms, and teachers of other subjects need to be redeployed to undertake this. Labour laws may be needed that will require otherwise redundant teachers to be retrained as English teachers. In addition, teaching English to young learners presents a special challenge since teachers of younger age groups often have a lower level of education than secondary teachers, and are least likely to have good English language skills. Several of India's challenges with regard to English language education are not exclusive but very similar to the experiences of other developing countries. What makes India unique is the combination of size and complexity. China is the only other developing country which can match India for size in both population and economy, however it has a completely different language situation in that it lacks a colonial legacy in relation to English, excluding Hong Kong, and educational decisions are taken in a different political context.

India is extraordinarily different in having built its recent economic growth on human capital, rather than on natural resources such as oil or on a low cost labour intensive industry like manufactured exports. There is a pressing need in India to improve the quality of education at all levels, and to broaden access to it. English has become the hallmark of a good education in India, for historical reasons connected to the development of the elite classes. Nevertheless English has now evolved to become a core part of the problem, by creating an unhelpful distraction from more serious underlying issues. The opportunities to learn and use the English language in Indian society, has traditionally been inseparable from access to privilege. Wider right to use to English is demanded by employers, parents, lower castes, in rural and urban areas alike. However there is also substantial evidence that, without care, a higher emphasis on English in education will permit only a few more to benefit, and possibly make the circumstances of the majority even worse (Graddol, 2010).

In the past few decades, numerous countries have made substantial investments in English teaching. The amount of investment in English teaching in China, for example, means that it can no longer be assumed that India will continue to have more English speakers than China. The reality of life in the subcontinent is that a little English will help maids, drivers and even a street beggar earn more, and it helps workers find jobs in neighbouring states although there has been little methodical research on the opportunities that English provides, or on what kind of English such workers might need. Astonishingly few large employers complain that there is a significant shortage of talent in India, which perhaps is reflective of the fact that the total number of jobs in the organised sector has barely increased during the recent two decades of economic growth. On the other hand, employers do complain about the growing burden of training and caution that if the services sector continues to develop as hoped, even the trainable pool may run short of supply. The education system in India must wake up and take responsibility for ensuring entrants to the workforce have good communication skills.

The mismatch between jobs and skills in India runs two ways. There are probably too few jobs in India that requires English or relevant higher levels of education to justify the investment being made in it by individuals, families and government. On the other hand, the important role English plays in finding work in the cities, and the magnifying impact of repatriation for education and employability has significant impact on the welfare of rural families. The geographical distribution of jobs is very uneven in a culturally diverse nation, nevertheless English helps overcome this by being a skill which increases employability and it is also a travel ticket by inevitably making job seekers more mobile.

The Indian Education sector needs to focus on developing spoken English skills, but the present curriculum, teaching methods and exams in the schools and universities are not set up to deliver this. Numerous educationists are concerned at the lack of any Indian exam which assesses spoken English proficiency. As Graddol (2010, p116) writes "The Central Institute for English and Foreign Languages (CIEFL) attempted to establish the National English Language Test (NELT), however found the difficulties insurmountable. Its successor, EFL-U, has now set up the All India English Language Testing Authority, (AIELTA), which trialled its first tests in 2010. However, the new AIELTA test will not assess spoken English." Major methodology, curriculum, assessment and pedagogical changes need to be implemented in the school and tertiary environment to keep up with English language skill demand. The introduction of continuous assessment in schools in place of centralised written exams that can be merely memorised and regurgitated, for example, may provide an opportunity for developing informal, school based assessment of a student's speaking skills. The intended use of Class 12 exams for university entrance will make it desirable to provide an assessment of English proficiency, in all four skills, to enable colleges and universities to know a student's capacity to study through English. If access to higher education is expanded, as planned, then secondary education may become a major focus for English language learning and testing.

English courses are now offered by the better institutions, these are too often focused on "employability" skills rather than study skills. Unless more university courses are taught in Hindi and regional languages, increased enrolment in higher education also implies an aspiration that at least 30% of the population acquires advanced English skills. The three language formula has long provided India with an educational solution to language diversity. However, it will need to be changed if levels of English proficiency are to be raised without lowering skills in other languages. Educationists and development agencies have long advised the use of the child's mother tongue as the medium of instruction in primary education. Rarely in educational circles has expert consensus on any matter been so consistent, over such a long period of time. Recent research has confirmed the importance of sustained learning in a first language, suggesting that children studying through English medium can suffer from an academic disadvantage for at least seven years even though they may achieve conversational proficiency in just two years.

No country can now avoid the need to nurture language diversity. It is an important factor in ensuring inclusive education, but is also an increasingly important economic resource. However, the debate in India seems still too focused on the question of which language should be the medium of education, rather than on how to create bilingual children. Developing a multilingual competence is not just a matter of acquiring linguistic skills. It is also about the development of communities and maintaining social cohesion through a period of rapid social change. Too often, school education creates a divide between parents and children, and a loss of traditional community values and indigenous knowledge. "The centre of gravity of the English language has moved from the native speaker to the non-native speaker" (Crystal 2008).

A major shift in the status of English in India is under way in the subcontinent. English will be used by more people, for more purposes than ever before. Graddol (2006, p. 14) the foremost authority on English Language in India, had this to say: "There are three main drivers in India towards the greater use of English: Education due to the increasing demand for English medium schools, widening access to higher education, incorporation of English training in vocational education; Employments since many jobs in the organised sector currently require good English skills; social mobility because English is seen as an access route to the middle classes and geographical mobility within India and beyond".

English has long been thought of as a "library language" in India but spoken English skills are now increasingly needed both for higher studies and employment. School curricula have not yet begun to reflect this change to a great degree, however the people and the government of India have begun to reflect that sustained economic growth requires more English speakers. The ambitious development road map for India predicts that the nation needs more people to move into the jobs in the organised sector which require English language skills. The rate of improvement in English skills is extremely slow and is not sufficient to achieve the needed rate of improvement in the English language skills of the Indian population. It is too slow to prevent India from falling behind other countries which have implemented the teaching of English in primary schools sooner, and more successfully. China may already have more people who speak English than India. The English language is a major casualty of the much wider problem that exists in the Indian education system. In spite of English having escaped from the library to the streets of India, students in many government and private schools continue to have very low levels of academic achievement and it is impossible to improve the standards of English without addressing the wider educational problem that exists in the system.

Chapter - 5

Research Questions

The research was conducted as a PhD study in The Faculty of Education, Monash University, Victoria, Australia, under the esteemed supervision of Professor Tony Taylor and Associate Professor Margaret Plunkett. Funding was granted through the Australian Postgraduate Award for research. The research investigated and tried to understand how the phenomenal growth of English language has evolved and to comprehend why it is continuing to occur and what are the major factors influencing English language growth in India? An attempt has been made to carry out the research to discover answers to these questions through the application of scientific mixed methods analysis.

The principal aim of this research was to examine the development of English language in the Indian education system and its relationship to India's growth into the largest English speaking nation in the world. It was intended to analyse through the views of teachers and educators covering the last 50 years. How this massive educational foreign language growth has evolved and what factors and issues have influenced and affected this transformation? Since it was a recent revolution, it was therefore an important topic of research to understand the nature of this social, intellectual and academic alteration in process. The research aimed to quantify analyse and examine perceptions of educators from different regions in India who were also teaching at levels from primary to university in different grouping situations in relation to their educational experience.

In the present study, the topic was one of immense social interest, the findings of which could assist in the understanding of a present educational dilemma, 'which methodology best assists in second language acquisition?'

Secondly there was also a pragmatic basis, as the topic had been chosen because of a keen personal interest. In conjunction with the importance of providing the most effective structure for answering the research questions, which was at the heart of the pragmatist's belief in "the dictatorship of the research questions" (Tashakkori & Teddlie, 2003, p. 20), a number of other considerations provided additional justification for the employment of a mixed method approach as an appropriate framework. A positive attitude toward bilingualism was an important factor in second language acquisition including resistance to the hegemony of English among non-native speakers. The educational arena was nevertheless the most important institutional variable in minority language maintenance (Williams,J. 2005).

Methodology

A mixed method of Quantitative and Qualitative study on mainly ethnographic grounds with an extensive library research for secondary sources in the fields of history, socio-cultural studies with an element of post-colonialism, education with regard to language acquisition and macro-economic impact was designed to deliver the answer to the key question. Quantitative research, in this case, involved the use of structured questions where the response options were predetermined and a large number of respondents were involved. After gaining ethics clearance, a field trip by the researcher to Indian educational institutions from 10th December 2008 to 26th January 2009 had given a survey respondent of 309 from different regions in India which was found substantial base for this research.

With such an environment it would take a lifetime to comprehensively survey all the states from the north to the south and east to the west. Due to time restraints this research had been confined to thirteen states in India with 309 questionnaire completed by individuals who were contacted through the phone in person and had questionnaire posted and given out to them. Of the 309 completed surveys, 167 respondents were from the southern most state of Tamil Nadu and the rest were from other states such as:

Utharanchal	-	8
Gujarat	-	8
Assam	-	10
Kerala	-	9
Kashmir	-	11
Andhra Pradesh	-	16

Maharashtra	-	9
Delhi	-	10
Punjab	-	8
Jammu Kashmir	-	10
Karnataka	-	48
Other	-	5

The subjects of the survey were educators from a wide range of teaching institutions and with an extensive array of teaching experience at primary, secondary and higher educational levels. The aim was to unravel the metamorphosis of the evolution of India's masses into Fluent English Language Speakers after independence. The participation was purely voluntary. The details provided would be combined with those of other participants. No identifying information about any individual was included in this combined data and data from the questionnaire was analysed statistically and anonymously unless agreeing to a follow up interview at the end. A scheduled questionnaire took about 20 minutes to complete. The questions were classified into participant's background, analysis of student progress and teaching methodology. The research aimed to quantify and examine perceptions of educators from different regions in India who were also teaching at levels from primary to university in different grouping situations in relation to their educational experience.

The survey involved measurement of perceptions, investigation of relationships between variables and exploration of those relationships to find answers to the different factors affecting English language acquisition and the varied influences they had in different situations. In quantitative terminology, the independent variables were grouped by ability while the dependent variables were self-efficacy, achievement, motivational orientation and attitudes to learning, which involved a number of subcategories. Much of the initial measurement of variables involved quantitative methods from data collected in the surveys which were supplemented and extended by qualitative data from interviews.

Proficiency in conversational language might affect the development of biliteracy, but the factors that affect bilingual proficiency were quite numerous and complex. Quantitative and qualitative research approaches on these factors by assessing the mixed research findings from the teachers feedback could unravel answers and implications for educational practices. The mixed method approach was most appropriate to the research questions and context of the study and more suitable than either a single qualitative or quantitative approach alone would be. A combination of survey research for mainly quantitative data collection and ethnographic research (interviews) were used. Provision of qualitative data was important due to limitations imposed by using one or the other to answer the particular research questions. A major reason for implementing a mixed method approach was that it allowed different types of research questions to be answered, for example, when one wanted to both confirm and further explore a theory.

Tashakkori and Teddlie, (2003) suggest "a major advantage of mixed method research is that it enables the researcher to simultaneously answer confirmatory and exploratory questions, and therefore verify and generate theory in the same study".

On the technical level, programs for the computer-aided analysis of qualitative data like SPS offered various combinations. Where the data were concerned, the employment of categories (for instance by using qualitative content analysis) allowed for combining qualitative and quantitative forms of data analysis. On the individual level, the creation of types and the inductive generalisation of cases allowed for proceeding from individual case material to quantitative generalisations. As for research design, different models were distinguished (preliminary study, generalisation, elaboration, triangulation) which combined qualitative and quantitative steps of analysis. Where the logic of research was concerned, it could be shown that an extended process model which combined qualitative and quantitative research could be appropriate and thus lead to an integration of the two approaches.

Further down the line after the quantitative data was analysed using SPS tools a qualitative research which was more subjective than quantitative research, using very different methods of collecting information, mainly individually with in-depth interviews was carried out. Participants were asked to respond to general questions to explore their responses and identify and define people's perceptions, opinions and feelings about the topic and idea being discussed to finally determine the degree of agreement that existed in the group. The data collected in the survey was sufficient to satisfy the assumptions underlying the range of tests which was eventually conducted. These included correlations to explore relationships between variables and t-tests and univariate and multivariate analysis of variance (ANOVA/ MANOVA) to explore differences between groups.

The use of two different methods were considered as one of the measures of strength in qualitative analyses, where researchers were encouraged to look for disconfirming evidences while it also offered an opportunity to more convincingly explain the social processes under investigation (Tashakkori & Teddlie, 2003). Finally, a mixed method approach to research the phenomenon of the rise of India into a Super Power with English language acquisition would substantiate what impacts the Growth of India into the largest English speaking nation in the world and how this phenomenon had evolved.

Chapter - 6

Data Analysis

Survey Data: Quantitative

Primary data was collected from 309 individuals for the study, of which thirteen or 4% had not indicated their gender. Overall there was a slight gender imbalance with females comprising 55% (169) of participants and males 41% (127). Participants' age ranged between twenty one and sixty plus, with just over 60% (190) between the age of twenty one and thirty nine. Table 6 outlines the details of age groups of survey participants.

Table 6 : Age Groups of Survey Participants

Age Group	*Frequency*	*Percent*
21-29	95	30.7
30-39	95	30.7
40-49	44	14.2
50-59	63	20.4
60+	7.9	3.8

Source: Empirical Data Computed

Participants worked in eleven main states within India, with just over half of the sample 54% from Tamil Nadu and another 15.5% in Karnataka. The other nine states representations were smaller as outlined in Table 7.

Table 7: Indian States Where Participants Worked

State	*Frequency*	*Percent*
Tamil Nadu	167	54
Karnataka	48	15.5
Andhra Pradesh	16	5.2

(*Contd...*)

Kashmir	11	3.6
Delhi	10	3.2
Assam	10	3.2
Kerala	9	2.9
Maharashtra	9	2.9
Punjab	8	2.6
Uttaranchal	8	2.6
Gujarat	8	2.6
Others	5	2.0

Source: Empirical Date Computed.

Qualification and Experience

With regard to the qualification of the participants, almost half 49% indicated that they held higher education degrees. The participants worked in tertiary educational institutions had a broad range of research degrees including Doctor of Philosophy; Professional Doctorates in Education, Visual Arts, and Music; Master of Philosophy; and Master's degrees in Higher Education, Social Sciences, Engineering, Arts and Science. 28% had Masters degrees which they attained purely through course work and were teachers employed in higher secondary schools. 14% of participants had only undergraduate degrees and were those who taught in secondary and primary schools while seven percent held graduate certificates in various disciplines.

The teaching qualifications of 18% of the educators who participated in the survey was a Bachelors of Education or Masters in Education. National Council for Teacher Education (NCTE) had clearly specified the minimum qualification for teachers in schools in 2001, as per the mandate under the National Council for Teacher Education Act, and also under the Right to Education (RTE) Act, which stated that all teachers appointed by the government or an employing authority should be formally trained and hold the minimum qualifications for different levels in school education such as pre-primary, elementary, secondary, etc. However, in alternative schools, which had been mainly established in slums and remote rural areas catering to underprivileged children, the mandate was not systematically followed. Teachers in these schools had been teaching without having the mandatory B.Ed., degree (Rogerson-Revell, 2007)). In relation to university lecturers, they were need not require to have formal teaching qualifications but postgraduate and research qualifications were mandatory for them.

In terms of teaching experience, varied widely amongst participants, with half of the group 50% had less than five years of experience while a third 33% had been teaching for one to five years. 17% were in their first year of teaching, while a 16% had more than twenty years of experience. The areas and disciplines which participants were involved in teaching are illustrated in Figure 5. In terms of the subjects taught by participants, just over 51% taught Science, 21% Arts, 13% Humanities, 11% Maths and only 1% Business and 3% did not provide any response.

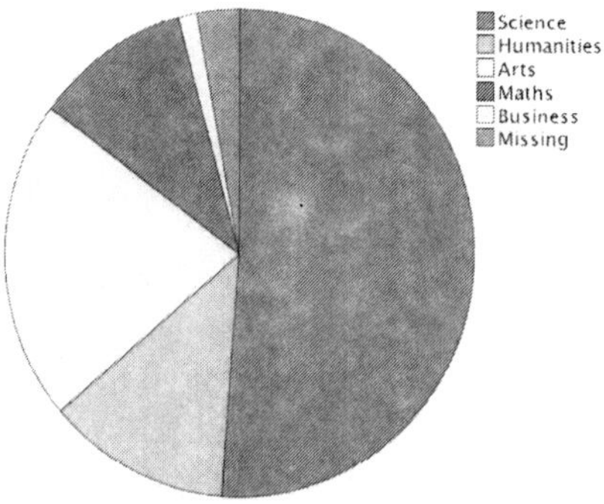

Figure 5: Participants Teaching Areas / Disciplines.

Among the educators who had participated in the survey, 146 (45%) indicated that they held a position of leadership in the roles that they were assigned to do. Between the educators who held positions of leadership, 14% were new to their positions for less than a year, 24% between one to five years, with smaller percentages held positions for longer with 8% between five to fifteen years and 8% had more than twenty years of teaching and of leadership experience in the Indian education sector.

English Proficiency

"Many Indians are bilinguals with fluency in more than two languages". This was also evident amongst the survey participants; with almost half 44% indicated that they were literate in Hindi, in addition to their mother tongue and English. 45% of the group were not literate in Hindi. This proved an important point for the analysis of data in the next section, as the Hindi literacy was utilised as a unit of comparison for opinions relating to English language proficiency. This was investigated as a possible source of difference, specifically whether participants with Hindi literacy viewed English language proficiency in the same way as those who were not Hindi literate. Figure 6 Illustrates mean sources analysing the participants English proficiency of those with or without Hindi literacy with the mean range of one to ten. Although the variances were not large, in every instance there was a higher level of agreement about English proficiency relating to those without Hindi literacy.

Since the official languages in India are Hindi and English and in most of the northern states, Hindi is the mother tongue, reliance on English is less when compared to the population in the South. In the southern states that were surveyed, as the mother tongues were usually Tamil, Telugu, Malayalam or Kannada, there was a reliance on English as the linking business language, hence overall proficiency levels to read, write, speak and comprehend English were higher M = 6.29 than among non Hindi literate individuals when compared to M = 5.58 in those who were Hindi literates. Similarly M = 5.59 claimed to be able to read English and not Hindi while only M = 5.65 could read both. Likewise, M= 5.96 could write English only while M = 5.63 could write both English and Hindi. The most significant difference was in speaking where M = 5.54 stated that they could speak in English only and not in Hindi, however only M = 4.83 could speak in both English and Hindi which confirmed that M = 6.29 were proficient enough in English to read, write, speak and comprehend it when only M= 5.58 claimed to be comprehensively bilingual in both.

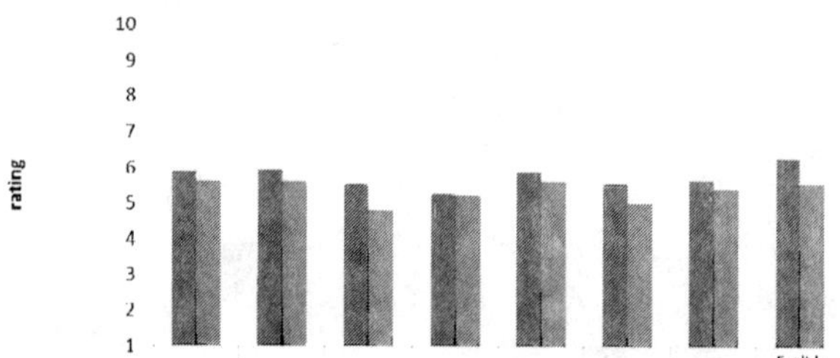

	English proficiency reading only	English proficiency writing only	English proficiency speaking only	English proficiency comprehension only	English proficiency reading & writing	English proficiency - speaking & comprehension	English proficiency - reading, writing & comprehension	English proficiency - reading, writing, speaking & comprehension
No Hindi Literacy	5.89	5.96	5.54	5.28	5.89	5.57	5.66	6.29
Hindi Literacy	5.65	5.63	4.83	5.22	5.63	5.03	5.42	5.58

Source: Empirical Date Computed.

Figure 6: Hindi Variance in English Proficiency.

Growth of English Language Proficiency

Almost two thirds 65% of participants expressed that English was studied as a compulsory second language in their courses, with 30% studied it as a first language and only 5% as a compulsory third language. 90% of participants indicated that English as a mandatory requirement in order to pass their courses, with 82% indicated that writing skills were assessed, while other skills were also considered important: speaking – 60%, reading – 57%; and listening 53%. More than half of the participants 58% said that students were allowed to use their local language or mother tongue in the class-room as with half of them 50% expressed that they themselves used the local language or mother tongue in their classes. The vast majority 81% indicated that they felt students found it easier if the local language or mother tongue was also used along with English. 257 respondents i.e., 83% agreed that there had been growth in the English Language proficiency within India, with 147 participants or almost half of the group 48% stated that they felt the growth in proficiency began around the year 2000. 19 respondents 6% felt that it had occurred from 1960 to 1990 but interestingly more than a third 35% of the participants had not responded to this question, suggested that they had not formed any opinion about the time frame for the growth. In terms of comparing the rates of English proficiency of current students with those of ten years earlier, there were differences but these were not statistically significant. The mean percentage considered to be highly proficient then was 32% while the figure for 10 years ago was 28%. In terms of not being proficient, the difference was even smaller during the survey period 24% and 10 years previously 26%.

Responses illustrated that the major factors perceived by educators as influencing English language growth in India were predominantly job opportunities. It was followed by the developments in Communication and Information Technology (IT) while other factors such as English being the second official language, media, globalisation, the education system also rated as other factors. Association of English as the language of the internet, knowledge of it bringing in elevation of status and it being a modern fashion trend in addition to being an international language with the western Christian missionary zeal, colonisation, being a commercial language and an international political and technology language also being stated as factors that have influenced the growth of English in India. Table 8 exhibits these results.

Table 8: Factors Influencing Growth of English Proficiency

	Factor	*In Number Figure*
1.	Employment / Job opportunities	60
2.	Communication	24
3.	Link language	8

(Contd...)

4.	Media	8
5.	Globalization	8
6.	Education System:English as Second Language	8
7.	Language of the internet	4
8.	Elevation of status	4
9.	Modern fashion trend	4
10.	International language	4
11.	English missionaries	4
12.	Colonisation	4
13.	Commercial language	4
14.	International Political Language	4
15.	Technology	4
16.	Population	4

Source: Empirical Data Computed

Participants were asked to rate their level of agreement (on a scale of 1-10) about factors they felt as affecting English proficiency of students. Interestingly all factors were seen as per the analysed data given in figure 7 with the mean range rate of one to ten having a fairly high impact of more than 7. The highest level of agreement was in relation to media influence with both questions attracting a mean rating above 8. The socio-economic context of the catchment area of the educational institution rated next M = 7.43, while language was viewed as less slightly influential with ratings for the mother tongue of parents M = 7.21 and local language spoken M = 7.16 below the other factors. Figure 7 illustrates these results.

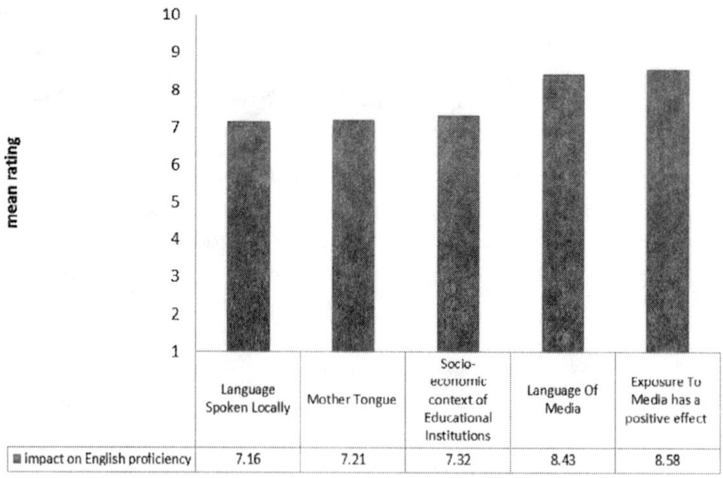

Source: Empirical Data Computed.

Figure 7: Level of Agreement About Influence on English Proficiency

Teaching Methodology Used in Tertiary Educational Institutions

Participants were asked to choose which of the following three methodologies they predominantly used in their classrooms – Didactic, Constructivist or Progressive. Significantly the Didactic method was chosen by most often as 39% with Constructivism slightly less as 32% and Progressivism still lesser as 24%, but this could have been influenced by the descriptors given for each method. Figure 8 illustrates the results.

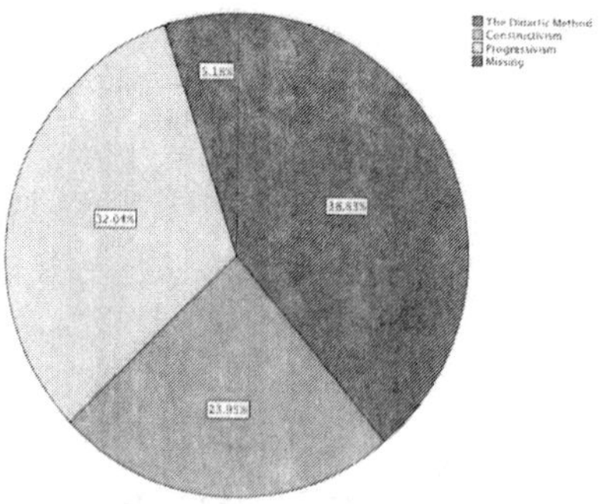

Figure 8: Predominant Teaching Methodology in Class Teaching

Participants were asked to outline which specific strategies they used in their classrooms. Small group discussions were the strategy that was most frequently used by two thirds 66% of the participants, with portfolios the least utilised 17%. These results are exhibited in Figure 9.

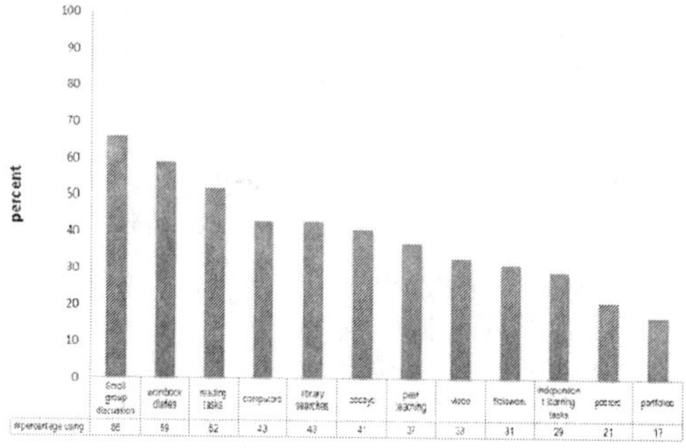

Figure 9: Teaching Strategies Used by Participants

Technology

Almost 85% of the surveyed respondents expressed that modern technology was available for them to use in their teaching. Over two thirds 71% felt that their initial attitude to using modern technology as 'enthusiastic'; while for 21% were 'willing to give it a go'; for another 7% had some reservations but only for 1% applying modern technology in teaching was 'resistant'. When asked to describe their actual adoption of new technology, innovations or processes, more than a third of participants 36.7% explained themselves as 'innovators', with just under a third 32.7% described themselves as 'early adopters'. Only small percentages of respondents indicated a reluctance to adopt new technologies as illustrated in Figure 10.

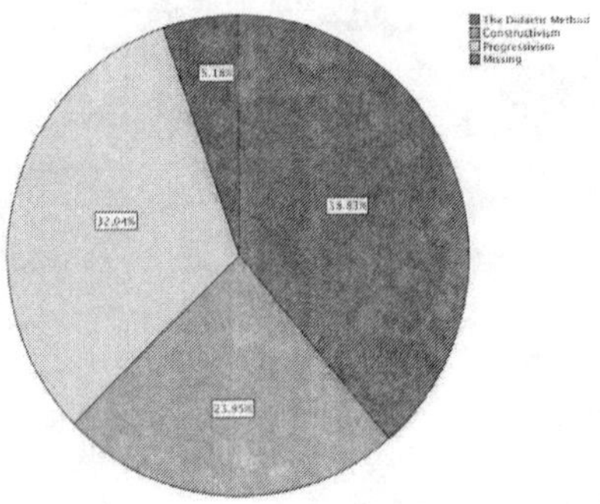

Figure 10: Initial Attitude to Using Modern Technologies in Course

Interview Data: Qualitative

The qualifications of the participants interviewed varied and was very diverse as depicted in table 9, so that the opinions and views of a wide range of individuals from different expertise were gathered. The level of experience and the positions of leadership that they held varied from young beginners in the teaching field to retired faculty who had been teaching for more than four decades and yet pursue research in their field of study. Table 9 also lists the various levels of experience and positions of the interviewed participants.

From Table 9 it could be seen that the qualitative analysis was conducted across all levels of educators from language teachers to science, management and technology experts with various levels of experience. Retired and fresh educators were interviewed to gain an understanding of what was being felt across the generations. The size of the class room taught also varied since there were senior academics who were guiding students individually through research degrees to lectures about hundred students and school teachers with approximately twenty five to thirty students in a class in primary schools while secondary schools usually had more than fifty students in a class. However, most undergraduate classes in the tertiary institutions had an average of thirty students in each class.

Survey Questions and Answers

Various questions were asked to ascertain what factors were felt to be influencing English language growth in the Indian subcontinent. To answer the question "Have you noticed any significant increase in English comprehension among students and have you noticed any growth in English language in India as a whole?", 17 of those interviewed which was 63% expressed that they did notice significant increase in English comprehension among students and that they noticed growth in English language in India as a whole. Only 7 of them felt that there was no significant increase in English comprehension among students. The reasons that revealed for the increase are listed in Table 9. Moreover twenty of the educators interviewed, 74% agreed that the number of speakers of English had drastically increased in India during the last decade.

Table 9: Factors Influencing Growth of English Language

Sl. No.	*Reasons for Increase*	*No. of Persons*	*Reasons for Increase*	*No. of Person*
1.	Awareness	4	Standard of language	1
2.	Interest	5	has come down	1
3.	Prestige	2	Government syllabus	3
4.	Job Opportunity	13	is not up to the mark	1
5.	Media	3	Rural Background	1
6.	Urban background	3	Dropped Studying	1
7.	Link Language	3	Not interested No reason	
8.	International Language	3		
9.	Globalization	1		
10.	Others	1		

Source: Empirical Data Computed.

Focusing on the research question on "what are the major factors influencing English language growth in India?", 63% reconfirmed that job opportunities as the driving force followed by other influencing factors such as technological advances as in the internet and cell phones, with media and other factors like English being an international language or link language, family background, personal interests, fashionable or trendy and status symbol.

Religion acting as a cause in some way or the other depended on the background of the home that held of individuals in India. With regard to the question on "if they believe that speaking good English gives additional prestige and status" 44% agreed that speaking good English gave additional prestige, respect and status. Hence the common theme arising was the desire among parents and students to learn the English language for better prospects. The next question was on educators "What is being done to build these English language skills and what is being focused on?" The teachers unanimously agreed that they encouraged students to speak only in English in the class and some schools, institutions have disciplinary rules in place to make students talk only in English on campus to encourage developing good oral communication skills such as listening and speaking in English which was found the prerequisite for any language acquisition. However a couple of educators still preferred the traditional methodology of focusing on training students to excel in reading and writing skills as a route to learning the language.

In addition, focusing on factors influencing English language acquisition, educators again unanimously agreed that the socio- economic background of the students affected their ability to learn English language. There were various socio-economic background factors and reasons stated that had significant impact on a student's ability to acquire the language skills which are listed in Table 10.

Table 10: Socio-economic Background Factors Influencing Language Acquisition

Sl. No.	*Reasons (Positive impact)*	*No. of Person (Some more than one factor)*	*Reasons (Negative impact)*	*No. of Person (Some more than one factor)*
1.	Economic status of the family ishigh	5	Economic status of the family is low	8
2.	Parents are graduates	4	First generation learners/ Parents areilliterate	8
3.	Students from Urban area (getlot of opportunity through media, school syllabus, etc)	3	Students from Rural area (don't get the opportunity)	8
4.	Medium of education at school level	5	Medium of education at school level	7
5.	Students studying in English medium in matriculation syllabus/CBSC)	5	Students studying in Tamil medium in Municipal/ Govt. schools	5
6.		NonAvailability of well trained teachers		5
7.	Regional	language/Mother tongue		5

Source: Empirical Data Computed.

Moreover 88% of respondents stated that they believed that their parent's education level influenced the student's ability to learn English. "Parental education is a must in the competitive world. It helps the student's ability to learn. Student's background will get affected because of the illiterate parents". Similarly with regard to the issue of media influencing language acquisition and affecting language growth, overwhelmingly 92% of respondents stated that the influx of free TV channels and the distribution of free television units by the government had accelerated the spread of the media across the subcontinent. This had contributed to English and bilingual programs infiltrating every household from the rich to the poor inadvertently motivating the youth to learn and communicate in English to be trendy and fashionable. In addition more than 50% of respondents agreed that the media motivated the children and youngsters to "Improve their English language, pronunciation, expression and learn phrases from English advertisements."

On the other hand, it was not only the electronic media but the print media too that continued to encourage language growth, in spite of encroachment of local language newspapers and channels. Teachers and academicians continued to promote English newspapers such as 'The Hindu, Indian Express and Times of India' etc., for reading. In addition, survey respondents who were approximately 30% claimed that television brought in the external wider world into their homes and created 'World Awareness' while students living in rural areas continued to prefer the local language media. Moreover only 8% believed that the media facilitated the development of high breed languages such as Tanglish (Tamil + English), Hinglish (Hindi + English), Manglish (Malayalam + English), Kanglish (Kannada + English) etc., as many international television programs being translated into the regional language to make it more popular among the locals. Besides 13% also stated that people were learning the language for business purposes.

Analysing the issue of religion, culture or any particular ethnic group in India being disadvantaged or advantaged in learning English, again overwhelmingly 80% agreed that no religion, culture or any ethnic group in India was disadvantaged or advantaged in learning the English language. However, 25% felt that Indian Christians had been exposed to more English through their church, sermons, and Bible readings and further encouraged to learn the preferred Christian language.

On considering the major issue of using the mother tongue in teaching, all educators unanimously agreed that the mother tongue was used by the students in the classrooms while 75% of the educators accepted that the mother tongue was used by the teachers in the classrooms along with English. The reasons given for the usage of the mother tongue by the educators in the class room were for explaining, clarifying and enabling the students to understand better. While 40%, also stated that they were not required to use the mother tongue in English Medium School classrooms. Moreover, only 13% of the educators felt that the students used the mother tongue in the classroom because of difficulty in expressing themselves in English with lack of confidence and shyness. Nevertheless, 13% also stated that the students from the science background were able to understand English better and had better comprehension of the English language when compared to students studying arts subjects.

Another significant issue studied was the teaching methodology adapted in the classroom by the educators towards teaching English, 43% claimed that their classrooms had interactive sessions with group discussion and assignments, role play and other activities. However 22% agreed that they followed the lecture oriented method since they had large number of students in every class. In addition 8%, that was, 2 educators confirmed that they followed the Montessori Method, or used the latest technologies such as e-learning and power point presentations. Another 8% stated that their teaching was progressive and constructive with only 4% claimed that they taught bilingually. Moreover another 4%, that was one respondent claimed that Chalk and Board method was used. Contrastingly another 4% respondents used almost all the methodology combined and mixed in their teaching. Specifically with regard to the methodology used for learning and improving writing skills one respondent affirmed that objective questions with multiple choices, fill in the blanks, short paragraph writing and essay type questions were applied in teaching and assessment.

In discussing the mode of assessments prevalent among the educators in India, 77% overwhelmingly agreed that written exams as the only method used to assess language skills hence soft skills were not usually applied. Only 8% claimed that they had systems in place to assess all the four language communication skills such as speaking, reading, writing and listening. Moreover merely 19% had the privilege to set or modify the teaching curriculum and 71% of the educators had no role in the syllabus, curriculum or assessment process but had to follow the prescribed syllabus given by the university or Central / State Government who granted the education system. In spite of the advances in technology and India being a major technology power house, only 15% who were 4 educators interviewed had access to technology that they could use to enhance their teaching and more than 78%, that was, 21 respondents had no access to any form of technology to assist them in the classroom. The qualitative and quantitative data had clearly defined job opportunities to be the driving force behind English language growth in India with an overwhelming majority acknowledging that there was a significant increase in English comprehension and English language growth among students in India as a whole. Various other factors such as technology, globalisation, colonisation, status, fashion trend in society, media, population growth, education system and higher education opportunities were other noteworthy issues that were raised as factors influencing the growth.

Moreover most educators and parents believed in the future of India with English as its unifying language and hence tended to encourage their students and their children to learn English for advancement in all spheres. However a vast majority were also inclined to believe that language growth was focussed mainly among the growing middle and upper middle class. But the economically backward sector lagging behind and missing out the benefits, students with educated parents had an advantage. The Qualitative and quant itative research through questionnaire and interviews conducted had provided valuable data that pragmatically found answers to the following research question.

1. What are the factors influencing India's growth into the largest English speaking nation in the world?
2. The English language has evolved to be the lingua franca of India.
3. Indian English has its own disposition because of the local languages and cultural influences and hence its evolution in the subcontinent has been distinct.
4. English is proving to be a medium for understanding technology and scientific development and language of political discourse, intra-national administration, international affairs and law, a language associated with liberal thinking.

The viewpoints of educators from diverse backgrounds, disciplines, regions and age groups was considered.

Chapter - 7

Factors Influencing Growth of English Language

Employment and Job Opportunities

The economic and social forces within the home country served to push students towards learning the English language for the betterment of their individual selves and their families' future since prime opportunities for employment were open and viable to only well accomplished and polished English speaking youth. With the unemployment rate as indicated in Table 11 indicated the unprecedented growth in the Indian population the unemployment rate has been steadily continued to rise and was in double digits which were very high for any economy.

Table 11 Unemployment Rate for India: 2002 - 2011-2017

Country	2002	2003	2004	2005	2006	2007	2008	2009	2010	2011	2017
India %	8.8	9.5	9.2	8.9	7.8	7.2	6.8	10.7	10.8	9.8	11.0

(*Source :* indiastat.com, 2012)

Hence people had to migrate one state to another, from villages to urban areas, and from urban areas to foreign nations seeking employment in various spheres. Moreover those who had good fluency in English language with excellent communication skills had been at an advantage for decades. They had always been able to do better. So the general feeling among the people was that English language should be developed and they should acquire the communication skills for the betterment of life and predominantly for improved job opportunities with the chance to acquire a higher standard of living and status in the society (Graddol, 2010).

Analysis of the collected data has revealed that individuals who were well qualified with communication skills in English got employment and hence, proficiency in the English Language in India was considered to be "a passport for employability". "One of our visions is we have to empower students towards employment". Considering the very high number of private education providers in India and the never ending demand for tertiary degrees, the vision of educators' needs to be considered and it is being implemented in the new evolving educational policies being drafted by the National Network of Education (NNE, 2011).

Moreover the interviewers confirmed that the major mode of recruitment among the major employing industries was through campus interviews as they provided a direct path way for the youth to employability in an environment where any work was found highly competitive. The recruiting corporate industries were always on the lookout for young fresh minds that had the ability to adapt to the modern world's new work ethics and rose to the challenges that might evolve. The study revealed "*When large companies come into campuses for* student recruitment, the only thing they asked for was to provide candidates who had good command of English. That is becoming a very *important and vital thing now in the present situation*". It also confirmed that at many of the campus recruitment interviews, candidates were being assessed on their communication skills in English by large recruitment firms hired from Business Process Outsourcing (BPO) network companies since communication skills are vital for successful survival. Also, aptitude testing was given in English and the recruiters communicated to the candidates in English. They entertained or accepted the profiles, bio-data, resumes of job seekers and students only if they were in English.

However another highly experienced educator reiterated in other words that "even in engineering colleges, the brilliant students those who are very good in communication skills are the ones getting good jobs in multinational companies. Average students without good communication skills in English are not getting good jobs. The motivating force is employability as well as salary." The same theory is reconfirmed by many who stated that "The Business Process Outsourcing (BPO) companies are outsourcing people. In the interviews the main thing that is looked at is communication skills. "Even the students who are not very good in academics but have excellent communication skills in English have the upper hand in job opportunities". This concurs with Dossani (2003); and Graddol (2010) who have argued in favour of BPO's in India and the significant effect they continued to have on the Indian economy and the growth of the English language in India which confirmed what most educators have said.

In addition it is a well-known fact that "*the remunerations offered* and bargained in these campus interviews tend to be on a much higher *scale to capture the brightest and best young minds.*" Furthermore, these interviews were all conducted in English only and good communication skills in the language were mandatory for any such opportunity. Hence the new trend had the youth on their toes to become proficient in the English language and was one of the main driving forces behind the growth of the English Language in India.

Another respondent stated that "*Employment opportunities have made English inevitable in India*". India has made a niche for itself in the outsourcing world. From low end work like data entry to high end research and engineering and medicine almost every level of skilled work is done in the country. India is renowned for its technical IT talent. It produces more English speaking IT graduates every year than any other country in the world. Outsourcing is a win win situation for everyone who is involved in it. America and other western countries including Australia get their technical and back office business requirements and services handled at much lower cost, while the workforce in India can reach global markets and improve its economic status. Due to the lower cost of living in India, the western companies are able to save hundreds of millions of dollars. The level of excellence India has attained in the outsourcing field has not been achieved overnight: a large pool of educated and versatile Indian workers, government support and innovative training techniques to help workers adapt to and emulate different accents have all played a vital role in India's success principally because Indians are inclined to learning and acquiring the English language skills required to attain this status and the jobs (Khokhar, 2006).

The teaching and training of English Language skills by itself is a booming industry in India today for employment. One informant stated that "*At the same time people are there to make money out of it. If you* know English, obviously you get a job or you can teach English in 'learn English in 30 days or 60 days' courses. You can employ yourself and create employment for many people. Hence it turns out to be two things under one heading. Attending an interview not only means that only communication skills are required but also many other skills involved: body language, decency, decorum, how to conduct yourselves, how to introduce yourselves, etc. Such skills are also imparted using English *language*"

India is a federal union of states comprising of twenty nine states and seven union territories with twenty two officially recognised languages. With English being the unifying language along with Hindi, those who want to become nationally employed would need English language skills. "*Now-a-days there is a lot of job opportunities in cities* and there are mass migration of people to cities from rural areas for employment. Initially when they migrate, they feel they are not empowered enough in the English language. They have high motivation to learn the English language through 'spoken English in one month or 2 months *courses*".

"*Even after being employed one's success in the work place totally* depends on how well he / she communicates. Subsequently whatever may be the job, the medium of communication in the work environment tends to be English among all outsourcing and international companies. As another respondent pointed out "You can't talk to a computer, so talk in *English*". "*Culturally parents play a vital role in their offspring's lives* throughout their life time, especially in the Indian culture. Henceforth private education in India is booming since it offers English as medium of instruction and then there is a very high demand from parents and students for life skills courses to equip them to successfully face the *challenges of the recruitment process*." This is confirmed by one private school educator who stated "*We are putting a lot of effort into teaching communication skills in English because of the demand*". "*Though* Indians take pride in their mother tongue and confine to it in their homes, the environment in the private schools are changing. Mostly people converse in their mother tongue. But in most private schools the students speak only in English on campus. So this helps students to communicate *well in English*."

Traditionally in the Indian academic environment, a student is not considered bright unless he excels in mathematics and science. Average students excelling in the international job market is mind boggling to traditional educators and it is transforming the way of thinking among current Indian educators towards the practicality of life skills like English communication skills and not theoretical learning of Shakespeare, Sonnets and Whitman.

"*The overall attitude of Indians in metropolitan areas is to learn* the English language for the purpose of survival. But this exuberance continues to be lacking in the rural areas of the subcontinent. This trend is magnified in the northern states that are identified as the Hindi belt. In such a situation English is the hurdle in which students are failing and leaving their studies without getting a degree. Some policy makers felt that the syllabus is burdening the students. Hence many *universities have started diluting the syllabus*". These issues had been picked up and discussed by Crystal (2008) and Kachru (1983) who have also identified earlier on the differences in the impact of the English language in metropolitan and regional areas of India.

Additionally, another academician confirmed by stating "*one* important factor is that India believes in villages and in its rural *community where the literacy rate is not high as in cities*". A large disparity in English language acquisition among the urban and rural population of the Indian subcontinent exist. One lecturer as well as a co-ordinator in a rural tertiary institution stated that "the ratio of the speakers of standard English and the kind of slang have increased while the competency in academic writing of English has gone down. A variation to slang business English is evolving with the number of graduates every year. Number of Indian universities have increased but the efficiency of the usage of the language has gone down."

Communication

The second most influential factor after job opportunities, that affected English language growth in India was communication as confirmed by 24% of the respondents. Vital communication skills in English is prefered for skilled work force (Bolton, Graddol, & Mesthrie, 2008; Martin, 2013). In addition it functions as a link language to communicate with twenty two official state languages and numerous other regional languages.

"*People migrate from one state to another and to countries* abroad. There is a lot of immigration to gulf countries and affluent people are going abroad for higher education and higher standard of living in western countries. Opportunities are increasing in the western countries due to the scarcity of population growth in the western countries like Australia, Finland, New Zealand and some European countries which have attracted the people with English language competency. Those who have good language standards and spoken English with communication skills are well off everywhere. So the general feeling among the people is that English language should be learned and they should acquire the international communication language for the betterment of life towards job opportunities, higher standard of living and to increase their status in *the society*."

"*Hence, large proportions of the population have to move* interstate or overseas for better prospects, employment or business. India being a multilingual country and with every state having its own state language, English has always been the uniting educational and business language for the subcontinent. Traditionally Tamil Nadu and West Bengal refuses to accept Hindi as their official language but voted for English as its second language as well. Moreover in all the private schools in Tamil Nadu, and elsewhere English is taught now. English is accepted as the official second language and international language. Recently English is being introduced in government schools as well. Even Hindi speakers feel the need to learn the English language because *they perceive that it is a universal communication tool*". English is the commercial language internationally and it is used in the international arena for negotiating political and international agreements. Without English, one cannot move around the world. India itself between its numerous multicultural and diverse states it is necessary to know English for communication. It is in the nature of man to be attached to the mother tongue. So it is very important to consider and maintain diversity of its various languages. English continues to play a very important role in the individuals and social life of individuals and in the political management of the states. States communicate with the central government and with other states for national integration and governance of the Indian subcontinent, which shows English is necessary for the vital functioning of its economic, political and other activities. Without it India cannot survive as a nation.

The fact that English is the language of business and communication in India has been found to be true, "*if you go somewhere* in India, like travelling to other states you should know Hindi to interact with the people. Otherwise English is used as the second language in all the other states. Only if you know English you can communicate there to do your business transactions or day to day activities which is one of the reasons for the growth of English. Good communication skills in English have become indispensable for the success of an individual in any field or avenue in the present day India. It has become essential in the lives of young people who aspire to advance their careers anywhere in the world. Being able to communicate well is the most important factor when seeking *a placement in a company or institution*". Communication involves one's ability to listen carefully so as to grasp the meaning and to respond in turn with apt words and clarity of pronunciation. These skills are being focussed on as India marches on forward into the new digital age (Samata,2012)

Link Language, International, Commercial and Political Language

The fact that English is now the main linking international language of business, trade, education, media or politics and accepted among most Indians as they have continued to see the growth across India even after seventy years of independence from the British. More than four decades back Quirk (1968) in his 'T*he use of English*'had argued that English would develop to be the linking language in the international, commercial and political world. Now it is spoken in many countries in the world by hundreds of millions of people and English is used in many signboards, tourist information and maps across India. Even leaders in international conferences and meetings use English when they transact, as English is the acknowledged current lingua franca of international business and air traffic control, and has displaced other competing European languages from this status.

The economic and political power advanced by the role of English speaking countries, in particular the United States and UK in the aftermath of the world wars. But countries like India have accepted it in the scenario of economic development. The position of English in the current world is that people are almost forced to learn English and use it, and learn it better" (Korpela, 2003, p.5). People travel everywhere and the students have opportunity to study in different places. So they need to know the international language like English. This is the main driving force. With the knowledge of English one can go anywhere in the world since everything has becomes global.

It is found that English is the commercial language in the international world of business. It is used by governments and in congress towards carrying out political, international agreements. Without English one cannot move around the world and in the same way in India itself as a multilingual nation this situation has happened. India is a diverse country and English is in the constitution itself, hence it is guaranteed that in India it will always have a position as the link language. Besides, if one language happened to develop as the national language and is accepted by all states internally in India, then English could be discontinued as a link language. This is one of the main reasons why in the beginning, seventy years ago when the constitution was framed by the leaders, it was mandated and English become the second national language. However, in the 60's the North Indian politicians wanted to make Hindi alone as the national language. Consequently massive anti-Hindi uprisings developed in non- Hindi speaking states against the imposition of Hindi becoming the sole national language. Subsequently, English is accepted as the link language in India along with Hindi. This is in order to maintain the unique character and richness of every states language and moreover India is divided by its state boundaries which have been marked based on the languages spoken in the areas and the role of the language there.

People are attached to their mother tongue and it is very important to consider the diversity based on the language. English does play a very important role in individuals' life, in the social and in the political management of the states. States communicate with the central government and with other states politically and commercially through English. What began for the purpose of national integration has served its purpose for more than seventy years. Now it is felt that English being the necessary language uniting the nation politically and economically and hence without it India cannot survive as an integrated nation. It is also stated that if it were not for English the southern states of India would not have developed into strong economic and technological power houses. This clearly shows that without having English functioning as a link, international, commercial and political language, India would not have reached where it is today in the global arena.

Media

Media in its various forms, through the centuries has acted as a vehicle for soliciting new world ideas and accelerated the adoption process of new ideas by engaging a new generation of speakers from across various backgrounds and ethnicity towards growth and evolution because of its adoption of the English language as its main means of conveying the message. In the present day, with social media skyrocketing in popularity, marketers across a range of fields and industries can devise strategies to achieve comparable levels of engagement using social media for their own purposes (Masani, 2012; Nayak, 2002). Media has continued to remain a driving force in the transformation of language and the expansion of its lexicon, dramatically reducing the amount of time it takes for new terms to achieve widespread adoption into various cultures. English as the language of the media is adopted and accepted by various language groups and in the process an inflow of vocabulary and phrases flow on backwards and forwards(Crystal, 2003). Any living language updates its vocabulary and grows to be vibrant.

Television

However, it is stated that it is only for commercial purposes that the media have adopted the English Language, aimed at making money. Moreover, most of the popular shows that are broadcasted on the local television networks are translated or transcribed as subtitles into the local language to increase its viewership and revenue. In Tamil Nadu the language adopted for telecasting are translated to Tamil, while for Andhra Pradesh it is Telugu, for Kerala it is Malayalam, for Karnataka it is in Kannada for many north Indian states, it is Hindi. In the Hindi speaking states they have so many Hindi channels with different dialects. Intermixing of English with reginal language is common. This is the way in which they also become more commercial while spreading awareness of English vocabulary, phrases and world affairs. It has been initiated and carried out for expanding business activities and hence it is a livelihood for many local cable network dealers who survive on telecasting shows in these languages.

Children are allowed to watch television in India very liberally since most shows are socially connected and the Indian cinema plays a great role in people's lives as they educate cultural values. Parents from educated families are using the television as an educational tool for their children to learn English. In order to improve children's English language skills, parents subscribe to English channels like the National Geography, Discovery, CNN, BBC, WION and other Indian channels of English which are popular among the middle class and the higher income group. These international television channels are now available in the regional languages for the lower middle class people everywhere. The channel organizers and TV companies are dependent on the advertisements for revenue. They gain profit through regional translation of the shows and telecasting them to everybody. "In spite of programs being dubbed in regional language shows like 'Dora the explorer' which is called 'Dora Booje',even in its translated version, introduces some English words like cat, mat, good morning, three letter words, four letter words, small words and phrases. This inadvertently allows the language learning even among the lower middle class and rural children watching regionally translated televisions. For the children to learn English in the classes, English documentaries are shown for one period a day. Normally one opens a book and reads but now people can visualise and also see what they have been reading, so they understand much better and are able to grasp the language faster.

Media plays a major role here through television but once again a comparison between the rural and urban areas needs to be considered. In the urban areas especially educated people can hear and understand the television news, the talk shows and the current affair dialogues in English, but in the rural areas students hardly understand what is happening on the screen. Most of them are exposed only to the regional language. So they prefer the regional language channels. In the rural areas the preference is for the local language channels where the visuals are taken from some other country but the background commentary is in the regional languages and sometimes English words are mixed. The urban people do watch English channels including BBC, CNN, The Times, CNN-IBN, NDTV 24X7, India Today, Mirror, Wion, NewsX, Discovery or National Geography. In the rural areas these channels are seldom used. But in the urban areas it plays a major role because they pick up words, accents, phrases or expressions from the English utterances.

Hollywood movies also play an important part. Moreover there is an element of continuous exposure to English through the media and there is a significant impact on the level of English language growth. Some of these English channels do have regional language versions especially Hindi, Tamil, etc. Hindi movies having English words and phrases in between the conversations, in spite of it not being proper English, still exposes the Indian masses to the language and makes it popular and fashionable to use such English phrases as a part of their day to day conversations. Hence they start speaking English inadvertently as seen through the popularity of a recent Hindi Bollywood movie called the '3 Idiots' where the phrase 'All is Well', 'All is Well' has become a common phraseology used by most Hindi speakers today. Though grammar and spelling skills might not be acquired, at least the communication level of individuals is being increased substantially through the media. As a result, there are both positive and negative influences because of the media. The media affects children in a very different way. It can influence both positively and negatively. It is positive in the sense that it makes children aware of different issues that exist in the outside world beyond their four walls. It affects negatively because it makes individuals put on certain masks in everything that they do, since it prevents them from being what they are actually, as they try to be more western and artificial by hiding their identities and adopting western values and ways. Some cartoons for children encourage violence and misadventure. "*One Indian education channels offer TV programs in* the morning for 15 minutes to 20 minutes where there is considerable *amount of teaching grammar and spoken English*." Hence it can be confirmed that media also plays an important role in language acquisition. Through TV general knowledge of children are enhanced.

The earlier view also affirmed that 'media plays a vital role in changing the children's perception of the local languages'. Some educated people watch BBC, CNN and other Indian English channels while those who are not educated watch the regional movies, regional songs and regional news, but the media is the one which changes the human perspective. A lot of importance is given to the Indian culture. Students learn more from the media and it can be clearly seen that it affects both the local language and the English language and it encourages English language acquisition.

The fascination over the western world has always existed in the minds of most Indians and recent developments have given the opportunity to see and experience it in their homes and learn to adopt and imitate the world they have dreamed off. It is the dream of many Indian to go overseas to learn or earn. The media has made it realistic and it greatly influence the people to learn English to fulfil their dreams. They are exposed to overseas events and focus on modern developments. TV is one of the medias dominating influence of the younger generation and at the urban level the impact is very high. It motivates and inspires a lot of the younger generation to imitate what is portrayed in the media. The media sets the fashion trends. Hence the language used in the media is believed to be fair and sophisticated that leads to be an inspiration for the youth of India to follow. On the other hand, in the rural areas, they switch over to regional channels is also occurring but they too imitate the English channels by imitating and copying from the western media.

Students find the Indian advertisements full of catchy English phrases which they adopt into their day-to-day conversations. Current affairs and popular talk shows which are predominantly in English, teach vital career skills such as how to interview people and how to answer in interviews. A good example was when Barack Obama had come to India, the questions asked by the youth were inspiring and how they put forth questions and how they got answer from him. It was found that the public and the youth were better at it than the professional reporters.

The electronic media has become an essential part of daily life. Electronic media has entirely besieged the developed and developing world. India is not far behind. Traditionalists believe that the media has introduced their thinking, priorities, social life and even their cultural and religious values because it is constantly feeding certain popular connotations and ideas which is eroding true Indian cultural values. These views have helped to a certain extent to protect the Indian culture and the traditional values.

Newspapers

India is currently the home of the world's largest English language readership of popular newspapers such as The Hindu, Times of India, Hindustan Times, Indian Express, Decan Harold, and the Mirror to name a few with other tabloids and a variety of localised editions which is not only healthy but is also expanding consistently. According to the Best Current

Affairs (2013), circulation is growing by a rate of 8% a year. There are an estimated eighty thousand individual newspapers, of which eighty five percent of them are printed in one of India's twenty two official regional languages, and the circulation of English language newspapers is expanding by about one and a half percent annually. Many non-English newspapers are growing three times as fast as about twenty million more Indians become literate each year (Auletta, 2012).

Though lifestyle habits, rising literacy and comparatively low internet penetration role, newspapers continue success and they have also built loyalty among readers by emphasizing their local identity in marketing there views. Deeply ingrained newspaper reading habits among the educated, characterizing elate values play a significant part in the industry's health, creating decades long relationships with readers. In India, reading the local news paper remains part of the morning routine, despite the growth of online news which is an urban phenomenon and if one could, he will move onto it until later in the day, at work. With fewer smartphones, tablets and computers than in western countries, it is less convenient for Indians to get their news online, besides the web versions of some Indian papers look flat, lacking interactivity and vivid images (Hayden, 2012).

"*When we were students in the nineteen fifties, we used to read* 'The Mail' and follow the media through newspapers. On the other hand, it is difficult for to read 'The Hindu' which is considered a bit high standard. However, these days it is not an exciting experience anymore to await for the newspaper to be delivered every morning, since they no longer publish credible articles as they used to be since we learnt the *art of writing from newspapers*". If students want to write competitive examinations they need to refer English newspapers for international news and to improve their general knowledge. This shows that it is not only the visual media but the traditional newspaper media that is continuing to influence language acquisition. Similarly for learning pronunciation most English language teachers continue to direct their students to listen English news channels, "when you want to speak correct pronunciation you have to listen to the radio or television news. In addition to that because of globalization, foreign channels are a great asset for Indians. Media plays a very important role in raising the awareness of people's rights and also what is happening around the world and comparatively on how India has to do much more to come up in the international arena. In the rural areas elders assemble near tea shops or temple shades to read and discuss newspapers. This is a common phenomenon in Kerala and Tamil Nadu in particular.

Advancements in technology and globalization of digital platforms and social media technologies are empowering people across the globe to participate, and share current affairs through the various forms of media available to them at their fingertips. India has been using the technology revolution as a vehicle in aiding social change through education and this has catalyzed English Language growth. The growth of the media is changing behaviors, perceptions, and attitudes as the ease and growth of technologies induce audiences to become digital activists; changing user behavior from passive to active, nonparticipatory to participatory, and enabling users with a voice that is otherwise unknown or untapped. The power of the media and its impacts on individuals, businesses, and society in India has provided an equal opportunity to voice thoughts, opinions, and share information. The increase of usage and ease of entry provides an attractive interface for anyone to become a creator or advocate of information and ideas by using blogs, micro-blogs, social sharing, and networking sites and these factors continue to accelerate the growth of English in India as all these activities happen in English.

Globalization

Globalization is a process of interaction and integration among the people, companies, and governments of different nations, a process driven by international trade and investment and aided by information technology. Globalization can be thought of as the widening, intensifying, speeding up and growing impact of worldwide interconnectedness. This process has effects on the environment, on culture, on political systems, on economic development and prosperity, and on human physical wellbeing in societies around the world (Beck & Camiller, 2000). Globalizat ion refers to the multiplicity of linkages and interconnections that transcend the national states and in the process across societies and cultures, which make up the modern world system. It defines a process through which events, decisions, and activities in one part of the world can come to have significant consequences for individuals and communities in quite distant parts of the globe. Goods, capital, people, knowledge, images, communications, crime, culture, pollutants, drugs, fashions, and beliefs all readily flow across territorial boundaries. Transnational networks, social movements and relationships are extensive in virtually all areas of human activity from the academic to the sexual (Berry, 2008).

With the development of communication systems, transport and other forms of technology, the world is becoming smaller and people are being required to interact with those outside their own language groups. This has a significant impact in the Indian scenario. Because of globalization, English has been established as the international language of communication. Furthermore, because of globalization there is a significant chance for it to expand across all borders and cross barriers. The countries like Japan and China have given more importance to the mother tongue rather than English but they started learning English due to the effect of globalisation. There is a demand for English teachers in China and it means only those who know English will be successful in the age of globalization. It is found that Indian teachers are preferred in Asian countries to teach English.

The most important factor and reason for the students to learn English is that it is a necessity for their future. Students are interviewed in English for education and career opportunities and moreover it is the unifying language throughout India and elsewhere. In spite of each state having its own language, English is India's unifying language and it is a global language. The world has become a global village. If anyone wants to go out of the country he needs English. Everything has becomes global. In India, there are so many languages but when the information is conveyed in English it has wider acceptance. The English language seems to give the impression of credibility and people seem to trust information conveyed in English than what is mentioned in the local languages. The impression is that globalization has made English more reliable than others because it is accepted as the language of the globe. Moreover the economic affordability of the growing Indian masses through the steady growth of Indian developing economy has made travel abroad affordable.

In an increasingly inter-connected world, the well-being of all people and the ability of educated members of society to contribute in alleviating problems such as poverty, hunger, women's inequality, social and economic inequity and exclusion, climate change, etc., must be a priority for institutions of learning. A Forbes article on 'Why Globalization is Good' notes, for example, that 'The booming economies of India and China – the Elephant and the Dragon – have lifted 200 million people out of abject poverty in the 1990s as globalization took off . . . Tens of millions more have catapulted themselves far ahead into the middle class"(Meredith & Hoppough, 2016). Education access has driven much of this transformation. As Wildavsky (2010) goes on to note,

"Today's swirling patterns of mobility and knowledge transmission constitute a new kind of free trade: free trade in minds." He summarizes succinctly the importance of globalizing our university campuses as "By eliminating protectionist barriers at home, by lobbying for their removal abroad, by continuing to recruit and welcome the best students in the world, by sending more students overseas, by fostering crossnational research collaboration, and by strengthening its own research universities in science, engineering, the humanities, the social sciences, and other fields, the U.S. will not only sustain its academic excellence but expand the sum total of global knowledge and prosperity" (Wildavsky, 2010).

And Why India?

In many ways India is the go-to place in South East Asia, in part because the student population there is globally diverse, the hunger for education at all levels is immeasurable, and the need for second language skills is minimal since English is the primary language of instruction and a commonly-used language outside the classroom. Studying in India also places US students alongside their peers from a number of other countries, including Afghanistan, Bhutan, Bangladesh, China, Iraq, Nepal, Malaysia, Sudan, the United Arab Emirates and several central and east African countries. Many from the latter countries immigrate to India every year to pursue education at the top universities in India at a tuition rate which is much lower than in other countries.

A-British Council report, for example, urges UK universities to partner with their Indian counterparts and warns that failure to do so will leave the UK significantly behind on globalizing: "UK universities must go to India if they are to benefit from a shake up to international higher education which will see India enrolling the largest number of students into tertiary education in the world by 2020," warns the report, as it urges British universities to move away from focusing on recruiting Indian students to forming partnerships in India, thus creating new opportunities for UK students and faculty to study and teach there and to collaborate on research.

India presents an especially viable opportunity because, for Indian students electing to study abroad, the US is the destination of choice, followed at a far distance by the UK and other English- speaking countries. The following represents the flow from India to other countries in descending order:

United States – 132,888, United Kingdom – 22,155, Australia – 16,150, Canada – 9,582, United Arab Emirates – 9,273, New Zealand– 6,845 (Smith, 2018).

Technology and Language of the Internet

Technology is the next most crucial factor influencing the growth of English in the subcontinent. With the birth of the computer and the entry of India into the digital arena, English is the language of electronics. Electronics, Software Writing, Computer Science and Information Technology have emerged as the most sought after courses to study in the twenty first century India. The Internet's revolution has changed the world, buckled cultural and ethnic walls, crossed international borders, and it has given new powers to individuals, people and nations. This Information Technology revolution has given a voice to many unheard and silenced voices and it has also presented a spring board for new ideas and views, whether they be controversial, accepted or not. English is adopted as the working common language of the Internet by its early builders and users as it was their language of expertise which has inadvertently led to it having become the lingua franca of the Internet. From its birth a few decades back to its evolution, market research companies are investing a great deal of money and time into discovering how people react to different Web page configurations and what makes a reader tick, the internet has come a long way. Today scientists and psychologists are beginning to probe the kinds of problem which affect individuals who engage in unconstrained fantasy play online and there is an enormous amount of "idiosyncrasy and variation seen in e-encounters" (Crystal, 2006).

The Internet's impact on the English language is irreversible as it has predominantly been promoting learning, democracy, and cultural understanding through efficient communication and bridging the gap between cultures and nations. The Internet is predicted to be a positive force for social change, cyberspace is a positive platform that is conducive to massive contact, community building, and language change and shift. As Indians are predisposed to acquiring knowledge the internet has been accepted as a library of information in spite of conservative fears lingering in the background of it corrupting the masses through its assault on their orthodox value system and way of life. Most educators agree that technology has played a significant role in the growth of English in the developing nations. In the 21st century India, many people have access to the internet and with the language of the internet being English it becomes mandatory that they learn English. Subsequently, until or unless they learn the language, they are not able to be in touch with other parts of the world and this is unavoidable since the world has become global. Moreover, there is a very high sense of awareness for learning, with a desire to learn, to fly the fabulant success. Indians know about what is competition in the world as they experience it on a day to day basis, they try to equip themselves and to run the race. Future will be much better if they have access and knowledge to use the internet. In some states laptops are distributed free to senior students in schools and all students in government colleges.

Students and teachers need knowledge and practice in using latest technology to survive in the competitive job market. It is a fact that the need to use technology and the availability of it is the driving force behind students and India's venturing towards learning English. Many people, especially the growing middle class have access to the internet. So their language has to be English since mostly it is the language in internet. Unless they learn English, they are not able to be in touch through the World Wide Web. English is the link language in spite of it sometimes degrade the cultural values, however the awareness or desire for learning to achieve fabulous success through knowledge and succeed in competition in the world, in the process equipping themselves to run the race so that tomorrow might be much better.

It is the internet that is the instrument behind this drive among the Indian population to learn the English language. English is considered the SMS language among the locals and the language of technology and progression. For survival in the information technology world the knowledge to communicate efficiently in the English language is a must. Because of the arrival of IT companies, the soft skills in English are also highly in demand with reading and writing skills. It is technology that has brought about a very large increase in English literacy in India.

Moreover, technology helps the people to spend time on reading. Normally one opens a book and read but now people can visualise and make up things from what they see. When one looks at the internet books, the written part on one side and the visual side on other. So one can understand much better. Both television and the internet are playing a major role in the development of English. In the academic year 2017-2018 the Tamil Nadu government introduced free tablets in 300 government primary schools. This has given a great boost to learn by reading and visualising the concepts without much pain for the under privileged children. The government of Tamil Nadu has proposed to start 3000 smart class rooms in government schools during the academic year 2018-2019. These classrooms could have electronic boards and computers for the students.

With the influx of call centres opening up through the use of the internet which has subsequently uncovered a conundrum of opportunities in the field of translation, transliteration, transcribing, telemarketing and customer support work. Training is usually offered through collaboration with foreign business schools to develop their English performance. In addition many tertiary institutions are providing students with laptops. Students get free laptops to study in government colleges as well. Students are encouraged paper presentations and to prepare the papers with their own laptops and towards working outside the box. Technology oriented education is slowly filtering in and gaining acceptance at all levels by traditional educators too. However, having access to a working internet connection is still a rarity in some remote areas.

Moreover, noticeably children studying in government schools have started setting up email accounts with enthusiasm and it motivates them to learn the language in order to use it. Their scholarship amount being deposited in the bank, it is found necessary to have a working knowledge of English. The basic thing that needs to be taught is email etiquette which would help students. In today's world one is literate only if he/she has computer knowledge.

In addition there are disparities that exist between the private and government institutions with regard to the technology facilities available for students and teachers. Private colleges are more equipped with modern technology than the government colleges, with facilities like language lab, computer lab, etc. Only a few of the government colleges are well equipped. Government colleges have to go a long way when compared to private colleges. Students from poor families cannot send their children to private colleges because students have to pay for every thing. It is obvious that great variation exist in the quality of education that is being offered by the private and government sector, due to social background of students, and different standards of teaching and their training programs. In the presence of great social diversity in India, it is difficult to change the social background of students, parents and their economic conditions completely. The use of Internet for education has a potential to change many aspects of lives in India as it can be used to enhance the quality of education in the country at all levels from primary, secondary to higher education.

History of Education in India

The British rule encouraged the formal education and higher education with English mainly to have trained Indians for their administration and consolidation of their rule. Extensive studies are already done on the nature of British rule and their educational policy for India. These studies point out the discussion between the 'Orientalists' or 'Classicists' and 'Anglicists' or 'Occidentalists' on education. The former group with leading personalities such as William Jones, H.T.Colebrooke and H.H.Wilson were concerned about the rich culture and values of India's past and the common link between Indian and Western culture. They were interested in incorporating the Indian richness into education and possing on the values to the generations. But the later group with Alexander Duff and Macaulay opposed the Orientalists in educational matters and tried to replace Indian culture with Western culture and promote the language of English. The Anglicists found the weakness of Hinduism and Indian culture and believed that the non-Western cultures need changes. So they brought some laws to introduce their system of education. One of the laws is the 'Downward Filtration Theory' (DFT) of Macaulay. Macaulay declared, 'It is my firm belief that if our plans are followed up, there will not be a single idolater among the respectable classes of Bengal thirty years hence'. This did not happen as he expected. Rather, many keep their culture, worship and spirituality and do not see any need to abandon them. The DFT did not transfer education to the bottom of the society but benefited only the upper and middle class people. Vast majority of dalits, tribals and women did not benefit by DFT. However, Macaulay's policy of making English as a 'bridge language' helped Indians to communicate within and outside India. Post- independence witnessed a tremendous growth of collegiate education. Christians and NGOs, added more schools and colleges and helping many poor people to get educated through their charitable service. Added to the growth of schools and colleges, technical and medical education developed to a height (Guanakan et.al., 2007).

The history of education is a vast subject. Education has gone through changes over the years. World is witnessing rapid changes in educational systems in the recent years due to the impact of information technology and globalization. Anyone who reads the newspapers in these days can notice several advertisements, both big and small in size, of the universities, colleges and institutes informing their programs, courses and degrees and inviting applications from students for admission. The variety of their programs is so attractive that students of present day have enormous choices to make for their education and career. This was not the situation a few years ago. A sudden growth of several institutions with multiplication of programs is a recent phenomenon. Another noticeable aspect is the advertisements of foreign universities from USA, UK, Australia and Singapore in Indian newspapers, opening their centres in different cities of

India for recruiting and giving 'spot admission' to Indian students to study in their universities. Of course, it costs a lot of money that ordinary middle class and poor families cannot think of such a study for their sons and daughters. This trend shows that overseas universities are now crossing their borders and education is becoming international and global. Some universities in foreign countries offer distance education program on certain subjects that Indian or African students can stay in their places and earn overseas degrees through internet facilities. All these activities happen in the English language.

The liberalization policy of the Indian Government has multiplied private and self-financing colleges. One of the main reasons for the policy of privatization of higher education is the lack of funds to support universities and colleges to offer new courses. State governments have instructed the universities to give permission to Private Trusts and Families to start self-financing colleges in their states. University Grants Commission (UGC) wants to reduce their grants to the universities and colleges since it is facing financial constraints. UGC has required the colleges to be assessed and evaluated by National Assessment and Accreditation Council (NAAC) to use its limited funds prudently to the deserving programs of the universities and colleges. These institutions, therefore, have to prove their excellence to get more students and grants from UGC. The scenario of education has changed very much since Independence.

Education System

The use of English in a variety of areas across the globe is a consequence of the reach of the British Empire. But the establishment of English as an international lingua franca after World War II was mostly a result of the spread of English via cultural and technological exports from the United States. English is also regarded by some as the global lingua franca owing to the economic hegemony of most of the developed western nations in world financial and business institutions. The de facto status of English as the lingua franca in these countries has carried over globally as a result. More Indians speak English than any other language, with the sole exception of Hindi, because of English being popularly taught as the second language in schools across India. Urban Indians are more likely to be multilingual but as many as 136.7 million rural Indians speak at least two languages (indiastat.com, 2012). Though the establishment of English as the second language in the education system has assisted in the growth of English in India, there are still many flaws in the system that need to be understood before one can completely comprehend how the complex and varied structure exists.

Flaws in the Education System

"There is a major decline in the standard of English among students. There were two universities in Tamil Nadu till 1965. Thanjavur district of Tamil Nadu in 1956 had only one college which was Kumbakonam Arts College that was then known as the Cambridge of South. Even though this is a government college where fees are expected to be moderate, however only well off parents could send their children to Kumbakonam Government Arts college. On the other hand with the changes in government policy, later education is made free in all government Arts and Science colleges. Hence pupils from all sectors of society have begun attending the college. Only top scoring students get admission in their preferred course. Others do not have any choice but are more dependent on chance in what courses they are offered to study. When the course that they are studying is based on chance, what it tends to lead to is they count the days towards completion of their degree and it is believed that educators have spoiled the education atmosphere to a very larger extent." In 2018, there are four universities and more than one hundred colleges for Arts and Science, Medicine, Engineering. Agriculture, Management, Education, etc. are established.

As per one professor "*The affiliating system is a wrong one.* Syllabus are set by the university and teachers are expected to teach without any academic freedom. They are not updated properly. When this is the situation the employability of the graduates is substantially affected. Under these circumstances frustrated youth are not interested in learning the subject as well as the language for business which is English. Another thing is language cannot be mastered over night. From the primary level planners have to initiate developing communication skills to the students and to inculcate this strategy by the teachers too. In Public schools and Matriculation schools the standard is maintained to a certain extent, but it is not possible for all parents to send their wards to these institutions. They are even not in the reach of salaried class and *lower middle class*."

The Indian education system basically promotes a rat race among the students without helping to develop the overall intellectual, vocational and social skills. The most apparent failure of the education system is that after completing graduation in any discipline, students are not suitable to most of the jobs. It is simply because skills that are required in a job market are not given. All that a student is taught in the schools and colleges are almost redundant for job markets. Hence educators and students are awakening up to the reality that it is not just subject knowledge but life skills with good industrial skills, practical skills and good English language communication skills that candidates benefit from.

Impressive Growth in Indian Higher Education

As per the UGC Annual Report 2015-16, the numbers have increased to 40 times in the case of the universities, 100 times in the case of colleges and the student enrollment has gone up to 165 times in the formal system of higher education in comparison to the figures at the time of independence. As on 31.03.2016, the number of universities stood at 799 universities – (44 Central, 75 Institutions of national importance, 342 State, 198 State Private and 140 Deemed to be universities) and 39071 colleges and 11923 stand alone institutions enrolling 34.6 million students as per the UGC Annual Report 2015-16. So far as the number of universities is concerned, Rajasthan tops the list with 70 universities, followed by Utter Pradesh 70, Tamil Nadu 52, Karnataka 49, Maharashtra 46, Haryana 38, etc.

But numbers alone do not suffice to earn India its repute in the field of Higher Education in the world. Serious concerns have been voiced repeatedly for utterly poor employability, acute shortage of well qualified faculty, lack of culture of research and knowledge creation, poor connect with industries and for ineffective regulatory system. The system is also least supportive of internationalization. The net result being that despite significant growth in the enrolment, quality, relevance and excellence remain as major challenges being faced by India's Higher Education system.

The FICCI report on Higher Education in India-Vision 2030 released at the FICCI Higher Education Summit in 2012 argues up that despite the fact that we are on the threshold of great opportunities to upgrade the quality and excellence "We are in the 21st century with a mid 20th Century Regulatory Architecture. During this time we have seen countries like China, Korea and Singapore, transform from developing to advanced economies in a decade due to strategic planning and a larger vision that correlated economic development to transformation in the education sector in particular higher education and research, to become globally competitive" (Sharma, 2018).

Education for Excellance

In a sector that has witnessed a lot of churn of late, including student unrest, the roster of excellence continues to remain stolidly predictable, with the National Institutional Ranking Framework (NIRF) India Rankings 2018 throwing no surprises. The third edition of the NIRF Rankings, released by the Ministry of Human Resource Development 2018 included overall rankings across disciplines and as well as category-wise ranking for engineering, pharmacy, medical, management, architecture, law, university and colleges. The Indian Institute of Science (IISc), Bengaluru, retained its position as India's top-ranked university for the third year in a row. Jawaharlal Nehru University (JNU) was ranked second, followed by Banaras Hindu University (BHU) in the third place (indiastat.com, 2018).

The top 10 in the 'overall' category (which considers all higher educational institutions irrespective of discipline) again had the IISc at the top and included six Indian Institutes of Technologies (IITs), with JNU in the sixth place and Anna University, Chennai, ranked tenth. IIT-Madras was first among the engineering colleges, IIM-Ahmedabad the best management school. AIIMS-Delhi topped among medical institutions. The Post-Graduate Institute of Medical Education and Research (PGI), Chandigarh, stood second among medical colleges and Christian Medical College, Vellore, was placed third. The National Law School of India University, Bengaluru, topped among law colleges.

Among colleges, Delhi's Miranda House stood first, while St. Stephen's College, Hindu College, and Sri Ram College of Commerce were the other Delhi Institutions to figure in the top ten, ranked second, fourth and seventh, respectively. Bishop Heber College, Tiruchi and Presidency College, Loyola College and Madras Christian College, Chennai, were the Tamil Nadu colleges in top 10. The NIRF rankings assess institutions on five parameters: teaching, learning and resources; research and professional practice; graduation outcome; outreach and inclusivity; and perception (Pathak, 2018). Study in India Website

Government of India has launched the study in India Website making the setting in motion launched the Study in India website, marking the setting in motion of an ambitious scheme to attract foreign students to study in good Indian higher educational institutions. The scheme will entail the admission of foreign students from 30 countries - with a focus on South Asia, South East Asia, West Asia and Africa to study in 160 quality higher educational institutions of India as per NIRF ranks and NAAC grades. With a large number of the available seats involving fee waivers, the attempt is to make quality education affordable to foreign students, as reported by the Higher Education Secretary, R. Subrahmanyam. The central education portal put in place for study in India is comprehensive, since students can register on it, they can apply for 160 institutions and get seats as per merit. It also has a provision for online counselling and a helpline number. The goal of the ambitious scheme is to increase the number of foreign students in India to 2 lakh by 2023 (The Hindu, 2018).

Teaching Methodology

Predominantly the teaching methodology followed in India in most schools and other institutions of higher learning is teacher centred and this is mostly due to the sheer volume of students. The emphasis in most Indian schools and colleges are on "exam oriented learning" which is the prevalent 'direct teaching' method also known as the "factory approach" according to Charlesworth, Hart, Burts, and DeWolf (1993) who agree that traditional mechanistic factory approach to education that has dominated elementary and secondary education is not working. It is not developmentally appropriate, culturally appropriate, gender appropriate, nor theoretically appropriate since it discourages students curiosity, questioning, innovation and feedback. This kind of teaching produces mechanical knowledge aimed at passing exams. Innovation in teaching and learning aimed at development of creative and original thinking skills are rare and if in existence, teachers find it very difficult to go beyond training students to pass exams to keep up their results statistics. Moreover, there is very little learning from first principles and cause-effect learning as few teachers and schools relate learning to actual phenomena's in nature, hence there is very little focus on application of knowledge and development of relevant practical skills.

In addition, the education system through its curriculum and syllabus that is required to be followed by the educators has very few incentives and opportunities for creative, collaborative and forward looking approaches for learning. Therefore teachers display a distinct lack of imagination and initiative in interpreting and enriching textbook learning as the assessment methods focus almost exclusively on exams. Many students would do better in class if alternative methods of assessments are factored into overall assessment. Moreover, off campus specialist tutoring courses is an accelerating and important phenomenon that has grown into a parallel education system. The tutoring sessions based on rote memory too totally focus entirely on exams and marks most of the tutoring classes are run by teachers teaching outside of regular work hours to supplement their income. This "factory based" approach to primary, secondary education and higher education combined with the race to secure a graduate and postgraduate degree has produced and is producing a large number of "graduates without effective thinking, application, teamwork and communication and leadership skills with far reaching consequences and implications."

The introduction of computers in high schools has not only benefitted students but also contributed to the introduction of different learning styles in the classroom setting. With the influx of foreign companies invading the subcontinent's shores, the lead-time for training and retraining new recruits in industry as well as the cost of such training is increasing since a large and growing segment of the population lacks basic vocational skills and requires basic training in social communication. Hence this inevitable leads to lower levels of productivity throughout the economic system which can accelerate expectations combined with a lack of productive opportunity, creating a potentially volatile situation for the employment sector. The explosion in graduates has not been matched by an increase in quality undergraduate institutions. This has resulted in fierce competition for limited seats in the reputed institutions which results in even a 0.5% difference in marks resulting in success or failure. For example, over 120,000 candidates compete every year for the 2,000 to 3,000 seats offered by the prestigious Indian Institute of Technology (Canagarajah, 2005). There are a number of aided private colleges that have high standard of education. But they cover not even 10% of the student population. In all these reputed institutions English remains the medium of instruction.

There is a provision given by the Tamil Nadu state Government that the students can write the subjects that they are specialising in the regional medium. Only the English language unit paper is required to be written in English. In spite of studying in the English medium they are allowed to write exams in the local language. Secondly they also say that those who study through Tamil Medium will be given preference in government appointments. In reality it proves just the opposite. However, the parents feel that if their children study through English medium, there is a kind of elevation in status, they feel prestigious to say that their children study in English medium. They feel proud when they see their children talking in English. Students want to communicate in English wherever teachers have started using Power Point presentations in class. For everything teachers have to depend on the English Language because technology is in English. So teachers say it is part of their life.

Many shopping malls came up in cities within 20 years. Many multinational companies look for student recruitment. They look more for communication skills than their academic skills. Their emphasis is not on academic merit but more on life skills. Private institutions prefer English to regional language proficiency. 'Add on courses', 'value added courses' are introduced. But courses for communication development are becoming compulsory. Professional development courses for the teachers are organized by the institutions to know how to handle new technology that is made available for teachers and students. Mostly trained teachers will deliver the professional development sessions and sometimes specialists or experts are invited to give lectures and demonstration. Refresher and orientation courses are given to college/university faculty.

"*It is claimed that using Liquid-Crystal Display (LCD) or flat* panels in the classroom helps a lot as students get motivated and excited about using it in the classroom. It is easier to get things across to the students and faculty feel that it is very convenient to teach using it. Instead of using traditional conventional black board method they find it much easier and also it is a great time saver. They are able to complete the syllabus easier and quickly using this technology. Opportunities for using this technology especially, in the teacher education training colleges are encouraging. There are, assignment program presentation and also web page evaluation. Hence for that session the students are asked to present their presentations using power point. This encourages them to learn, practice and gain confidence in using the technology. In addition when students enrol for training in Information Technology they are provided with laptops each. Therefore all the 100 students who are enrolled have laptops.Subsequently, for paper presentations laptops are used because in future they have to have the *skills to use technology as a part of teaching*".

With developed India in the 21st century, the explosion of knowledge has rendered the term 'up to date' redundant. Knowledge is changing so as that only 'up to-momentness' or up to-fraction of a moment' is in. In such an era only fit societies or institutions, having an ability to 'adopt', 'adapt' and 'being adapt' might survive. Information and Communication Technologies are potentially powerful tools for educational change and reform. When used appropriately, it can help expand access to education, strengthen the relevance of education to the increasingly digital workplace, and raise educational quality. It will help make teaching and learning into an engaging, active process connected to real life situation.

Necessity for Technology in Teaching

In this information era, education is greatly influenced by two major developments: increasing use of information technology and forces of globalization (Vrasidas & Zembylas, 2003). Technology has facilitated education, and interaction takes place on a large scale and over long distances. The teaching methods and styles have undergone tremendous changes due to new technologies integration in the class room. Classrooms today in developed countries are equipped with computers and other technological equipments that aim to enhance the learning experiences. A few decades earlier, educators had begun discussing the impact of learning technologies in that period. The technologies that existed previously were different from the technologies that are used today. The same technology has continued to grow and new learning technologies are constantly evolving through discussions and research on the impact of new learning technology on classroom dynamics, which still has a long on going journey ahead for educators. Besides, recommendations for school transformation along with technology mediated teaching innovative practice have been expressed in many countries (Chan Lin, Hong, Horng, Chang, & Hui-Chuan, 2006). Technology innovation and dynamics changes redefine how to teach and learn in the intersection of theory and interactive tools (Provenzo, 1999). A combination of constructivism and interactive technological tools such as social networking and interactive white boards is one model for innovative teaching practice. From the perspective of constructivism, learning environment constructing for students is a key to facilitating students' learning. The combination of constructivism and interactive technological tools, therefore, enable teachers to create learning environments that promote interactivity and realize teaching goals.

Web technology such as social networking sites and mobile hardware have contributed to this generation change (Teclehaimanot & Hickman, 2011). Mobile technology and hardware enable learning to happen in a timely manner. Today's mobile phones are like "small computers" in their own right with the capability of internet searching, information downloading and uploading, and its most popular among students: convenient applications downloading and implementation from app store. These 'small computers' make interaction happen through texting or other applications. Learning technology is not a new concept. Textbook based curriculum is a curriculum that tends to be boring and uncritical. Papers, pens, typewriters, projectors, computers, internet, mobile phones and social networks have been an innovation journey for the classroom learning tools. Even though there have been new technologies introduced into classrooms, however, classroom challenges have remained essentially the same: how can we use the technologies at our disposal to impact classroom interaction, and then to improve both teachers and students' classroom experience and learning outcomes. It is widely accepted among teachers and researchers that learning becomes more effective and meaningful when it takes place within an appropriate environment that displays real world attributes (Westera, 2011). A vast literature on integrating "real world" environment into classroom suggests that learners must acquire underlying knowledge and concept maps instead of simply memorizing facts and techniques. Classroom technological tools such as Interactive White Board support the "combination of interactive teaching and interactive learning" (Sessoms, 2008). In addition, Learning technologies help teachers and students access more web-based curriculum, which means can start to work and view on a subject or topic together in front of their own computer rather than face to face. In the education system of India all these technological activities are happening in English language.

Learning happens anywhere and at any time; information sharing does not stop after class or out of the classroom since learning and sharing can continue. However, pedagogical context and practices are deeply grounded in tradition and routines are being reconstituted with the influences of technology development. Friesen and Anderson (2004) support the theory that lifelong learning associated with profound flexibility, in which learning is encouraged to happen anytime, anywhere in anyhow, is able to be adressed with the support of web technologies. Similarly, Beldarrain (2006) reveals that since the emergence of new technology, curriculum designers and educators have unique opportunities to foster interaction and collaboration among learners, thus creating a true learning community. Mobile technology provides support for students to work collaboratively through network, rather than only work with allocated peers in a fixed venue. The fact is that teachers are learning about education software at the same time as the students do. This synchronous learning makes the relationship between students and teachers even more equal.

Nevertheless, when it comes to usage of Internet, online learning competes with entertainment, social networks, e- commerce, news and many other things. Moreover absence of internet penetration in rural areas poses a barrier for companies to reach out to the rural masses and unavailability of bandwidth also hinders interactive programs like virtual classroom connectivity and live streaming. In addition, rural people are less susceptible to change as their mindset is geared towards a traditional classroom setting (Mehta & Mehta, 2012). As technology becomes more affordable and investments in the education sector are increased, the English language will continue to grow among the masses as it has always done since it is a channel of communication and knowledge.

The impact of technology on higher education is phenomenal as it has added a new dimension to teaching. As of February 2017, there are 789 universities, 37,204 colleges and 11,443 stand- alone institutions in India, according to the latest statistics from the UGC website. So one cannot expect Indian institutions to grow further to accommodate 400 million students knocking at the portals of the colleges. And even those who graduate are not career worthy or employable. To speak about loss of jobs in such a scenario sounds anachronistic as the number of jobs in existing colleges will remain the same. Again in a vast multilingual, multicultural and multi-religious country like India, education has to cater to students of different regions speaking different languages. While the study material is prepared, it has to be not only in English and Hindi, but in multiple languages. The video capsules have to be made similarly in many Indian languages. This again requires a large number of teachers to write the course material in different languages and prepare the video capsules.

Technology Revolution

Technology revolution has impacted every aspect of lives, more so the education system. Information and Communication Technology (ICT) pooled with Liberalization, Globalization and Privatization (LPG) have accelerated the pace of change to jet speed. As per the data on the Net, the Mobile usage rate is more than 88.0 percentage in India which is more than the literacy rate in the country which, as per NSSO data is 74.4 per cent. It indicates that the Mobile phones are being used extensively by the people in general irrespective of their educational status. It also indicates that the technological gadgets like mobile phones are conducive for usage even for non-literates. Most of the mobile activities happen in English language.

In the process of usage, many people are seeking education informally. Thus, the awareness level among the masses is increasing exponentially. As per the Ministry of Human Resource Development report (indiastat.com, 2018), tertiary enrollment rates in India have increased at a compound annual growth rate of 3.5% in the five years preceding 2016. Current enrollment stands at 34.58 Million, over 15% more than the 29.2 million enrolled in 2011. Evidently, the 'Aspiration Rate' of people to seek higher education also is on increase day by day, which in turn is creating tremendous pressure on universities to provide affordable and attainable higher education. The universities therefore, have to realigning their roles through reforms and innovations to meet the demands of today's fast changing world where educational possibilities are endless. Robust and judicious use of

Disruptive Technologies and Disruptive Innovations can come to the aid of Indian Higher Education system to cope up with the situation. Through Disruptive Technology, India can make higher education more accessible, attainable and affordable thus serving as a bridge to fill the gaps between the 'Haves' and Have Nots'.

Disruptive Times : Challenges and Opportunities

India is witnessing a disruptive era of social and technological changes. Globalisation of economies and technologies has brought significant changes in life, work and play. Internet and mobile technologies have significantly 'disrupted' daily lives of people. Artificial intelligence (AI) and robotics are about to 'invade' the homes and lives. Several social changes have become equally disruptive:

- Rapid migration from rural to urban areas
- Disruption in joint family system, individual ahead
- New social norms of communication
- Consumption for now, not for tomorrow.

Social responsibility emerges as the need to reconsider the social relevance of universities in light of the encounter of the local with the global, regarding priorities, demands, impacts and knowledge needs in the context of globalization. The competitiveness of nations – as the only way to achieve progress – should be balanced with inclusive social development and sustainability of the entire global population (Tandon, 2018).

Elevation of Status and Prestige

English has special national status in India. It has a special place in the parliament, judiciary, broadcasting, journalism, and in the education system. "the small proportion of people using English corresponds to the social class which is tightly integrated to world economy and techno-structures"(Montaut, 2010). One can see a Hindi speaking teacher giving his students instructions during an educational tour about where to meet and when their bus would leave, but all in English. It means that the language permeates daily life. It is unavoidable and is always expected, especially in the cities. An Indian who knows English does not hesitate to speak in that language with a foreigner, who is anticipated to know the language. For instance, an Indian dignitary who knows English would readily converse in English with a visiting foreigner or deliver a talk in English at an international forum. This can be contrasted with the medium that delegates or dignitaries from other countries use in similar circumstances. Other than in exceptional scenarios, English knowing Indians do not usually have any antagonism towards English but on the contrary it is deemed to be of high status to be able to speak in English. But it creates problems where linguistic fanaticism exist. Many time the English TV channels use Hindi without any hesitation.

The importance of the ability to speak or write in English has recently increased significantly because English has become the de facto standard. Learning English language has become popular for business, commerce and cultural reasons and especially for internet communications throughout the world. English is used widely by people from higher strata of society. As a result find a wide percentage of Indians who are multilingual and take pride in talking in English whenever and wherever possible. English remains the no longer the language of the elite and moreover the only trans-regional, trans-religious language, that is, supposedly able to transcend local chauvinisms and group interests. But English continues to remain the only language creating unanimity all over India in secondary schools as it is English and not Hindi which is the language of government and administration (Montaut, 2010). Whatever the field of specialization, there is no doubt that being educated in English is a great advantage for practical purposes. Up until the 1960s South Indians were better in using English. Of late, North Indians whose mother tongue is Hindi, Have caught up with the South Indians, since the need of the hour is better felt by the North Indians as well.

Parents encourage and motivate their children to speak in English. When tiny kinder or preprimary children are taught to speak a little bit of English it tends to fill their parents with pride. Speaking in English is respected and believed to be knowledgeable. It is considered of a very prestigious language. Prestige and employability are the major factors influencing the population to learn English. This theme of gaining prestige and being considered elite and of a higher class because of the communication skills in English is rampant and it prevails all over India, across all communities and classes as it is thought of as a ticket to upliftment.

In the cities like Delhi, Bangalore, Chennai, Calcutta or Hyderabad, there are good instructions that give opportunities to develop their language skills. In the meantime, India believes in its villages and it is the rural community that are the life blood of the nation, however the literacy rate is not high as in the cities. When parents are educated, they can talk in English with their children and hence they pick up very fast. If they are in good schools and if the teachers are good, then they develop good language skills, accents, on the other hand if the teachers are not skillful then the children suffer.

The socio-economic background plays a very crucial role in English language acquisition. The society can be divided into three: high income group who usually are political big wings, and the aristocrats, big business people, technocrats, industrialists, etc. The middle class can be divided into the lower income middle class and higher income middle class. Even among the middle class, higher income middle class includes the professional people, professors, doctors, politicians and service oriented businessmen, the higher income people are in a very high status in society. They control and run most of the daily affairs. Low income middle class outnumber the other two groups, consisting of middle level government employees, teachers, business men and the educated middle class. Government employees and nonprofessional people earn reasonably a good amount of money for their survival and on their own. Lower strata of the society are the majority in India. However, the low income people are very poor and moreover the poorest of the poor, small farmers are dalits, tribals and indigenous people who live in remote areas. The schedule castes, schedule tribes and the most backward community people are dependent on daily wages and they tend to work as house maids, servants, day to day construction workers, laborers, etc. All three categories of people are aware of developments in India and the need for English for their upliftment. Most of the present day Indians inspite of their class differences take pride in sending their children to English medium schools.

Indians everywhere have the aspiration to come up in life with English. Maid servants and the under privileged strata of society like to send their children to English medium schools at least for primary and secondary studies. Earlier on, even if they could not pay for higher education still they aspire to rise the status of their children. However due to the low quality of English teaching in normal schools the standard of English has come down. Middle class people also prefer English medium schools to regional language schools. Higher income people can afford to send their children to the most privileged residential schools which are very expensive and are out of the reach for others. Lower income group and the middle class have to study in government schools and colleges and their opportunities are very limited and competitive towards getting admissions to sought after courses in medicine, engineering and the Indian Administrative Services category as they have to write the entrance exams.

However, most of the government colleges in Tamil Nadu are also of exception standards where the University Grants Commission is meticulous in appointing qualified faculty members who are remunerated competitively. Very rarely do public school students succeed in getting admissions based on merit into the course of their choice and preference. In rural areas, the government schools are their only options and private schools are not available. Nowadays government schools in rural areas do have qualified teachers and they perform well to raise the standard of their students. Moreover, the rural people cannot send their children to urban centres to study since it is financially and geographically difficult for their children and inevitably they have very limited options for higher education.

To have equal opportunity for all strata of society and to avoid discrepancies in admissions and to balance the disparity there is a quota system. Quota system is set up to favour the schedule caste and schedule tribe people who can benefit with opportunities to educate their children. Reservation of seats for the backward class is also given by the government where certain seats are available in proportion to the population for the schedule castes, the schedule tribes and the backward classes. This has been set up to correct the inequalities between the rich and the poor and the caste divide. Equal opportunities are available on this basis to uplift the poor and to influence the English language growth.

Even in rural colleges, English is the medium of instructions in addition to regional language medium. Regional languages have not yet developed to impart higher education in science, engineering, medicine and other especially technical subjects. Books and reference materials for research and other facilities are not available for professional courses in regional languages. Students have to know English, otherwise they cannot study professional courses. In a culture where dignity, self-respect, honour are valued and prestige is sought, the English language provides them opportunity to bridge the class divide through education. Where English communication skills are encouraged and taught parents sacrifice everything for their children to have respect and prestige and feel delighted to find their children speak in English and get recognition.

Contribution of English Missionaries

The introduction of English to the Indian linguistic landscape opened with the dawn of the British colonial era in the early eighteenth century and contrary to the most popular pre- independence consensus, that Hindi would dethrone the English language after independence. English has not only continued to flourish in the educational and official network of India but has also become one of the official languages of the nation and thus continues to enjoy the patronage of the Indian elite. There is no doubt that British imperialism had a large impact on India and one of the most important factors in the British loss of control over India was the establishment of English as a unifying language, having previously been a group of independent and semi- independent princedoms and territories. Prior to British colonisation, India was fragmented and disintegrated with 15 major languages and around 720 dialects (Burton, 1998). English served as a common ground for Indians, and allowed separate cultural and ethnic groups to identify with each other, something which had rarely if ever occurred before on a grand scale. Although it was mainly educated Indians of a privileged class who spoke English, they were the most influential people in terms of acting as facilitators for nationalist ideas to be communicated throughout the populace. This knowledge of principles such as autonomy and freedom naturally led to many Indians desiring this for their own nation, understandable since it appeared that the world's greatest and most powerful nations were self-governing democracies, and this system was obviously successful.

The success story of English has been due partly to the nature of the language, but more to the fact that it has developed into a mature national language. The seeds for the establishment of English education in India were sown by British missionaries who had set up English medium schools to sow the seeds of faith and pull the suppressed underprivileged castes out of poverty and discrimination through love and education. This is widely acknowledged and still accepted as one of the factors that has influenced the growth of the English language in the subcontinent. English missionaries started many schools where English was the medium of instruction. As the seeds of faith grew English was identified as the language of the Christian religion and the converted Indian Christians. Christians particularly have taken up every opportunity to educate their children in Christian schools which the British started in the early days and many of them had very dedicated teachers. Initially they also had to learn the local language and so they wanted to make sure that what they taught was understood by the students (Verghese, 2010). Their influence was not only in the schools but through their lifestyle, faith and ministry particularly in churches by conducting Sunday school programs among the children, they converted the locals to their religion and their way of life which sowed the seed for English language growth among the locals.

Most of the Roman Catholic and Protestant Christian missionaries who came to India to spread not only the gospel but along with the gospel they started many charity organisations such as hospitals, vocational centres, cottage industries and schools. In the schools, English was taught and much importance was given to the language. Children who were educated in the missionary schools and with parents who had converted and those who were growing up in Christian households gained substantial advantage of being exposed to, encouraged and motivated to learn English than their other counterparts that led to social transformation.

It is true, as per the caste system in India, the people belonging to the high castes in the social strata have inherited the advantage of learning English. They worked for the British and gained much favour in learning English. They also guided their children properly to come up higher in their lives by educating their children in English. However, people belonging to the middle class professionals were usually the Anglo Indians and Christians who had the advantage of learning the English language. During the fifties and sixties, in the Christian institutions, students were not allowed to even speak in their regional languages on campus. They had to speak only in English. That was the motivating factor among the children to learn English. On the other hand, later that kind of enforcement did not exist. Due to lack of opportunities children have to go to spoken English classes and communication skills classes to learn life skills in English. There are a lot of private coaching centres that have developed and during the holidays children are sent there to develop vital English language communication skills. If children read the newspapers, listen to various English TV channels, it will have a great impact on them towards developing their communication skills in English. Without the work done by the Christian missionaries in India, India would not have the advantage that it does have today when compared to some of its other Asian giants. If not for them many Indians would not have been able to dig their ways through education and language acquisition out of the hierarchy of the caste system that had defined and ruled India for centuries.

Christians Contribution to Printing Press of India

It was Christian missionaries, who endeavored to translate the Bible into the regional languages of India, introduced printing and publishing in the country. In fact, India acquired its first printing press in 1542 through Francis Xavier, a Spaniard, who taught the Bible in Tharangabadi (Tranquebar), Tamil Nadu. Likewise, when the Viceroy of Goa, on behalf of King Joan III of Portugal, opened schools for Indians and printed books, the press stayed in Goa and was set up at the college of St. Paul in Goa (Verghese, 2010). The huge arch of the St. Paul's College gate, restored by the Archaeological Survey of India, stands as a witness to this pioneering effort.

If the location of the earliest printing in India were plotted on the map, it will be found that they were all located along the coastline of peninsula India, Goa, Cochin, Pinnaikkayal (Near Kanyakumari), Vypicottai (Near Kodungallore) and Ambalakkadu (Near Thirusur), Madras (Chennai), Fort William, (Calcutta) and Serampore along the east coast representing the shaping of Indian printing. Bombay contributed its share towards the second phase of the vigorous growth of early Indian printing. Roman Catholic Mission and the Protestant Mission from Europe fathered and furthered this impulse in their anxiety to translate the Bible and thus spread the Word of God and the growth of English in India.

Boost to Literature

The start of printing in Goa spread along the southern coast and its attainment of maturity at Thrangambadi (Tamil Nadu) has been described as the dawn of printing in India, but the sunrise in all its brilliance was when William Carey set foot in India on November 11, 1793. The Bengali alphabet inprint form became a reality. The Serampore Mission of Carey was a pioneer in this respect, helped by William Ward and Joshua Marshmann, establishing a press in Serampore in 1800. Two able Indians, Pachanan Karmakar and Manohar helped in casting the types, publishing in 40 Indian languages, for the first time. Carey also set up the first papermaking factory and the first foundry in India.

The introduction of printing and the consequent development of the languages of India had a tremendous socio-political impact, leading to enlightenment and empowerment. The second half of the 19th century began to witness a change from the old to the new, from the medieval to the modern. A scientific new educational system was being launched and practices like Sati (Widow burning) and infanticide were abolished (Verghese, 2010). 'Publish or perish' is an old saying. It is true even today as Missionaries contribution by introducing printing technology which is a forerunner to modern developments in world languages in general and English language in particular.

Chapter - 8

Future of English Language in India

English Integrates

With the developments in the communication systems, transport and other forms of technology, the world is becoming smaller and people are required to interact with those outside their own language group and English has proved itself as the global language. English is a language that has become a standard not because it has been approved by any 'standards' organization but because it is widely used by many information and technology industries and recognized as being standard (Graddol, 2010). The call center phenomenon has stimulated a huge expansion of internet related activity, establishing the future of India as a cyber technological super power. Modern communications, videos, journals and newspapers on the internet use English and have made 'knowing English' indispensable.

The prevailing view seems to be that unless students learn English, they can only work in limited jobs. Those who do not have basic knowledge of English cannot obtain good quality jobs. They cannot communicate efficiently with others, and cannot have the benefit of India's rich social and cultural life. Men and women, who cannot comprehend and interpret instructions in English, even if educated, are under employed. They cannot help with their children's school homework everyday or decide their revenue options of the future. A positive attitude to English as a national language or link language is essential to the integration of people into Indian society. There would appear to be virtually no disagreement in the community about the importance of English language skills (Davidson, 2007). Using English today in most parts of the world gives anybody the right to become a citizen of the world almost naturally as English plays a dominant role in the media.

It has been used as a medium for interstate communication and broadcasting both before and since India's independence. India is without a doubt, committed to English as a national language (Graddol, 2010). The impact of English is not only continuing but increasing.

Can India Become a Great Power?

India is often spoken of as a great power in the same breath as China because of its billion plus population, economic promise, value as a trading partner and growing military capabilities. This is seen as a misconception by many as there are very few similarities between the two Asian giants. As forecasted by The Economist (2013) "Although poorer and less economically dynamic than China, India has soft power in abundance. It is committed to democratic institutions, the rule of law and human rights. As a victim of jihadist violence, it is in the front rank of the fight against terrorism. It has a huge and talented Diaspora. It may not want to be coopted by the West, but it shares many western values. It is confident and culturally rich. India is well placed to provide security in a critical part of the global commons. That India can become a great power is not in doubt. The real question is whether it wants to".

Asian historians would testify to the fact before the 19th century, India and China were the world's economic super powers. Thanks to their new economic rise, they will soon regain their former status and our perceptions of the relative importance of world languages may also change (Graddol, 2006). The world economy is experiencing impact of two new economic super powers emerging simultaneously. Together with Brazil, Russia and South Africa they form a group referred to by economists as BRICS. The BRICS summit displayed a distinct nonwestern tendency by acknowledging the important role that Chapter – 7 Future of English Language in India.

English Integrates

With the developments in the communication systems, transport and other forms of technology, the world is becoming smaller and people are required to interact with those outside their own language group and English has proved itself as the global language. English is a language that has become a standard not because it has been approved by any 'standards' organization but because it is widely used by many information and technology industries and recognized as being standard (Graddol, 2010). The call center phenomenon has stimulated a huge expansion of internet related activity, establishing the future of India as a cyber technological super power. Modern communications, videos, journals and newspapers on the internet use English and have made 'knowing English' indispensable.

The prevailing view seems to be that unless students learn English, they can only work in limited jobs. Those who do not have basic knowledge of English cannot obtain good quality jobs. They cannot communicate efficiently with others, and cannot have the benefit of India's rich social and cultural life. Men and women, who cannot comprehend and interpret instructions in English, even if educated, are under employed. They cannot help with their children's school homework everyday or decide their revenue options of the future. A positive attitude to English as a national language or link language is essential to the integration of people into Indian society. There would appear to be virtually no disagreement in the community about the importance of English language skills (Davidson, 2007). Using English today in most parts of the world gives anybody the right to become a citizen of the world almost naturally as English plays a dominant role in the media. It has been used as a medium for interstate communication and broadcasting both before and since India's independence. India is without a doubt, committed to English as a national language (Graddol, 2010). The impact of English is not only continuing but increasing.

Modern India and the English Language

India is one of the emerging superpowers of the world, together with China and Brazil. Nonetheless, what sets it apart from its major economic strategic competitors such as Japan, China and Brazil is its status as the growing largest English speaking nation in the world. This is an interesting advantage for India especially in a world where English is the lingua franca. It has the second largest population of "fluent English" speakers, second only to the U.S., and is expected to have the largest in coming decades. At the same time, in India, English has a status of 'link language' (Daniel, 2007), but it is the most important language of India, since, after Hindi it is the most commonly spoken language in India and probably the most read and written language in India.

English has permeated some of the most important parts of society; the government and civil service, the media, the education system, the legal system, and gradually the social sphere as well. India is recognized globally for its vast talent pool of English speaking, well educated professionals because of these tactically introduced political policies (Khokhar, 2006). From being a language rooted in colonialism, English has become the language that has given India an edge over countries where English is a foreign language. India has become a resource pool of multilingual, proficient English communicators whose ascendancy remains unquestioned. English plays an important role in the domains of education, administration, business and political relations, judiciary, industry, etc. and is therefore a passport to social mobility, higher education, and better job opportunities. Indeed, in urban India, it is very common to see young people code mixing and code switching between English and other Indian languages.

Once independence was won and the English were gone, the perception of English as having an alien power base changed; however, the controversy about the role of English has continued to this day (Crystal, 2008). Since then in the present day India, English now has national and international functions that are both distinct and complementary. English has thus acquired a new power base and a new elitism (Kachru, 2004). Moreover, only about three percent of India's population speak English as a first language, they are the individuals who mostly lead India's economic, industrial, professional, political and social life. Even though English is primarily a second language for many, it is the medium in which a great number of the interactions in the above domains are carried out.

India and Common English Usage

Despite being a three percent minority (Baldridge, 2002) which should be significantly more though no current accurate statistics exist, the English speaking population in India is quite large. When considering India's massive population, that three percent. India among the top four countries in the world with highest number of English speakers. English confirms many advantages to the people who speak it despite the strong opposition it receives periodically. Nevertheless, having such important information moving in English is not often appreciated by Indians who do not speak it. It is more readily accepted in South India, where English serves as a universal language in the way that Hindi does in the North.

In India, where more than 22 different state languages coexist with English serving as the connector between people speaking these different mother tongues, the phenomenon of the conqueror's language as link language continues to evolve even after 71 years since the British left. So more than two hundred and fifty years later, the number of Indians who wish to learn and use English is still growing steadily. The impact of English is not only continuing but increasing. The number of English newspapers, journals, and magazines are on the increase and as Crystal (2008) affirms, British English is numerically speaking, a minority dialect, compared with

American, or even Indian English. In fact, Indian English is a recognized dialect of English, just like British Received Pronunciation or Australian English, or Standard American. It has a lot of distinctive pronunciations, some distinctive syntax, and quite a bit of lexical variation.

Indian English morphology is very creative and it is filled with new terms and usages. Indians also shorten many words to create commonly used terms. The Indian English lexicon has many distinct terms which are commonly used by its speakers. Some arise through the use of old and new morphological features. Others come from acronyms and abbreviations. Many terms from Indian languages are utilized and new usages for English words or expressions are created. It must be noted that many of these terms and usages are specific to the population of Indian English speakers who are between twenty and thirty years of age. New words and new usages of standard words are introduced as well. (Baldridge, 2002). English is widely regarded as having become a Global Language, but will it retain its pre-eminence in the 21st Century? Chinese, Mandarin has more first language users than English, Hindi / Urdu, Spanish and Arabic are close behind English. On the other hand, how secure their place will be in the third millennium is a matter of speculation.

Languages in multilingual areas are often hierarchically ordered in status. To the extent that such relationships are institutionalised, the hierarchy can be thought of as applying to countries as much as to the repertoire of individual speakers. Higher up the pyramid are languages which are found in more formal and public domains and have greater territorial "reach". Graddol (2000, p12) Figure 11 depiction of the language hierarchy of India in 'The Future of English' clearly exemplifies the status of the various languages in India. It is to be noted that only Telugu, Tamil, Kannada and Malayalam belong to the Dravidian family of Languages. All the other in the scheduled languages are from Indo Aryan family of languages.

Where English has a place alongside other languages in a local language hierarchy, speakers normally use their first language in different contexts from those in which they use English. Whereas the first language may be a sign of solidarity or intimacy, English, in many bilingual situations carries overtones of social distance, formality or officialdom. Where two speakers know both languages, they may switch between the two as part of a negotiation of their relationship as they would tend to switch between both the languages for example, Tamil and English, in a way which only a member of the same speech community can fully understand. It is amongst professional groups that the use of English is most prevalent and professional

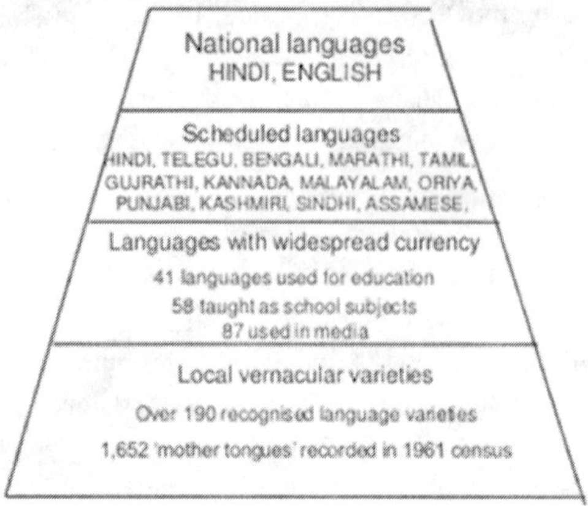

Source: Graddol (2000).

Figure 11: Language Hierarchy in India.

middle class families are most likely to adopt English as the language of their home (Graddol, 2006). Urbanization is likely to have wide reaching effects on the world's languages. New languages emerge, others change, some are lost. In the world's cities the nexus for flows of people, goods and ideas with the spread of English will be felt first and most keenly; new pattern of English use will arise amongst second language speakers. The projected native speakers for major world languages in 2050 as estimated by Graddol (1997) Table 12, provided by the engco model in millions forecasts what to expect.

Table 12 – Estimated Speakers of Major World Languages in 2050

Language	No. of native speakers globally (millions)
1. Chinese	166.0
2. Hindi/Urdu	73.7
3. Arabic	72.2
4. English	65.0
5. Spanish	62.8
6. Portuguese	32.5
7. Bengali	31.6
8. Russian	14.8
9. Japanese	11.3
10. Malay	10.5

Source: Graddol (1997)

Will the Spread of English Lead to the Extinction of Many Small Languages?

One of the main challenges facing many countries is how to maintain their identity in the face of globalization and growing multilingualism. There is a case for regulating the status of English but ways need to be found of reinventing nation's identity around a distinctive mix rather than a single language which is kept pure. The need to protect the national languages, and scheduled languages in India is to ensure that English does not intrude or unnecessarily take over too many domains. Public communication, pedagogic and formal genres and new modes of communication facilitated by technology, may be key domains to defend (Graddol, 2006). The global spread of English may also be associated with decreased use of endangered languages.

Some linguists in the developing world do connect English with inequality. English is backed by international groups which treat English as an instrument of colonization and as a commodity of trade. It interprets skill migration as brightening life chances and it accentuates the divide between the rural and the urban, the developing and the developed, and the elite and common masses. It permits better education for a miniscule minority. At the same time, it inhibits interaction between science and society and it inhibits the creation of appropriate technology (British Association for Applied Linguistics, 1996).

The social consequence of English medium education often reflects local, political and cultural histories and differing colonial legacies. In India, English has been accused of being associated with social elite wishing to maintain its privileged position. A parallel can be drawn between English as a colonial imposition supported by a segment of the elite and receiving a stiff nationalist opposition and on the other hand, the current imposition acclaimed by a segment of the population aspiring entry into the elitist privileges and opposed by a larger segment of population (Graddol, 1996). One of the reasons why English education is such a sensitive matter in many countries is because, the distribution of English proficiency may affect the balance of power and negate regional languages and disturb ethnic groups and for that reason be subject to political management. Migrant and minority communities tend to gradually lose their ethnic languages and adopt that of the majority community. The loss of at least 50% of the world's languages means that the remaining languages will acquire native speakers as a faster rate than population increase in their community. As regional language hierarchies become more established, there will be a shift towards languages higher in the hierarchy (Graddol, 2006). The changing status of languages is expected to create a new language hierarchy for the world as depicted in Figure 12 (Graddol, 1996).

In comparison with the 2013 hierarchy there are more languages in the top layer. Chinese, Hindi / Urdu, Spanish and Arabic may join English. On the other hand French, German and Japanese are likely to decline in the status. Nonetheless the biggest difference between the 2013 language hierarchies and those of the future will result from the loss of several thousand of world's languages.

The Big Languages Chinese, Hindi / Urdu, English, Spanish, Arabic
Regional Languages (The languages of major trade blocks) Arabic, English, Chinese, Malay, Russian, Spanish
National Languages Around 90 languages serve over 120 small states.

Source: Graddol (1996)

Figure 12:
New Language Hierarchy

Culture and the English Language

Surveys indicate that in many ways, Indian English is unique (Baldridge, 2002). Its distinctive characteristics are etched into the cultural life of Indians, and it is very much a part of the familiarity of being Indian, even if the individual is an expert, literate or familiar with the language. Most Indians are of the impression that the use of English should be keenly encouraged because of the many benefits it confers and the greatest of which is its universal character. The Indian writer and philosopher Raja Rao wrote:

"Truth, said a great Indian sage, is not the monopoly of the Sanskrit language. Truth can use any language, and the more universal, the better it is. If metaphysics is India's primary contribution to world civilization, as we believe it is, then must she use the most universal language for her to be universal. And as long as the English language is universal, it will always remain Indian.... It would then be correct to say as long as we are Indian-that is., not nationalists, but truly Indians of the Indian psyche - we shall have the English language with us and amongst us, and not as a guest or friend, but as one of our own, of our caste, our creed, our sect and our tradition" (Kachru, 2001, p. 12).

Many others fear, perhaps legitimately, the loss of India's native languages, (Baldridge, 2002).

English has changed Indian languages in many ways, mostly through the incorporation of new words. However, the population of English speakers in India, though socially influential, remains a small minority. Also, most of these individuals are conversant in at least one, if not two or three, other languages, and unless the situation necessitates English, they usually speak in their native language. It seems that multiple languages can function together when they each have their particular domains of use (Baldridge, 2002). The sheer number of speakers of India's native languages more or less ensures that they do not face extinction. However, English is still in a slightly precarious position. Although it has a strong base in the elite class of India and in the general culture, it could easily fall victim to an anti-English movement if one ever arose. Public fervour is known to be especially forceful in India, and a skilful leader could use it to create such a movement. Hopefully, this will not happen. Indians have a lot to gain from knowing English, and the world has a lot to gain from Indians knowing English. Some Indians complain that English brings in too much Western culture and thought, but English in India also exports a vast amount of Indian culture and thought to the rest of the world. This increases the diversity of experience that people around the world receive as part of their education. Rather than worrying about whether or not English should be used, people may choose to focus on extending an education to more children which allows them to learn and use English, but which also puts a great emphasis on using and understanding their native languages.

English language is being spread in India by the world of work and, most interestingly, young India is gearing up to meet the challenge of English. An analysis by the Indian Express, a leading national daily newspaper, on the Indian Retirement Earnings and Savings (IRES) shows that nearly forty percent of the young earners in the age group of twenty to thirty have at least a rudimentary ability to read English (Graddol, 2010). Bearing in mind over the last hundred and fifty years, more particularly in the post 1945 period the question now rises, What is the educational background of 21st century India's position as the second largest English speaking nation in the world? More precisely, how far has India's education policy and practice recognised the commercial and geopolitical value of English to India as a nation? This question might best be answered through an examination of the changing experiences and attitudes of a representative sample of Indian educators at work over the past 40 years. On the face of it such an examination might best be tackled using both Quantitative and Qualitative methodology, called mixed methods by academia, to analyse their responses.

Josh Marshall quotes the following from an interview with Peter F. Drucker who was a writer, professor and a management consultant and often called the man who invented management argues that India may be a greater economic power in the future than China. Josh Marshall excerpts an interview with Peter Drucker in which he claims

"I've long believed that India rather than China would be the nation to eventually supplant the United States as the world's leading superpower, for three reasons: Firstly, English is a main language in India, which would make a transition from American primacy to Indian primacy easier just as the British to American transfer was aided by a common English language, and the French to British transfer was aided by a common knowledge of French. Secondly, India has maintained the British legacy of democracy and relative freedom and tolerance, which, combined with the recent loosening of state controls on the economy, makes India more likely to foster innovation and change than China. Third, because of the two reasons already stated, Americans would be more comfortable ceding leadership to the Indians - people with whom we have important attributes in common - than we would to China" (Drucker, 2006).

India has gained from knowing English

English is still in a slightly precarious position. Although it has a strong base in the elite class of India and in the general culture, it could easily fall victim to an anti-English movement if one ever arises. Public fervor is known to be especially forceful in India, and a skillful leader could use it to create such a movement. Hopefully, this will not happen. Indians have a lot to gain from knowing English, and the world has a lot to gain from Indians knowing English. Some Indians complain that English brings in too much western thought, but English in India also exports a vast amount of Indian culture and thought to the rest of the world. This will increase the diversity of experience that people around the world receive as part of their education. Rather than worrying about whether or not English should be used, people should focus on extending an education to which more children which allows them to learn and use English, which in turn impact to higher input for emphasis on using and understanding their native languages.

English, many claim, is now an 'Indian language', as it provides access to a better life to previously disadvantaged strata of the society. At the morphological level English language has made inroads in all the South Indian languages such as Tamil, Telugu, Kannada and Malayalam. The national language Hindi has spread its tentacles due to centre part patronage in the Indo Aryan family of languages of North India with the exception of Bengali and North Eastern states where English is dominant. In the meantime, English has the additional advantage of being the link language of India uniting the Dravidian and Indo Aryan family of languages. Hindi as a national language has gained as a first language in North India, where as English as a second language expanded more in both South India and North India as well as North East India. Unwritten languages may suffer at the growth of both English and Hindi.

Globalisation has been a swifter than expected process which has increased communication and interaction between the nations and its public. It has bought about rapid increase in the movement of people, money, services, goods, ideas, information and opens up opportunities for the entrepreneur. The internationalisation of education is an important contributor to the growth of a global knowledge society in which concepts, views and information move rapidly around the world, crossing countless borders in the process creating a unified globe where information can be accessed at the touch of one's finger tips. In a globalised society and economy the ability to communicate across cultures, with others, assumes greater importance than ever before. Those who were once far away become neighbours, and the cultural and economic survival depends on them whilst also being threatened by them. The effects of globalisation are undeniably evident in all aspects of higher education ranging from the development of economic and political strategies for institutional and national educational growth to a focus on individual learning designs for students (Hellstein & Reid, 2008). Support in developing the knowledge and skills of local students about global processes both by embedding them in core curriculum and in providing co-curricular opportunities to learn emphatic communication life skills with English language acquisition will see Indians develop further as a formidable nation and power house in the global sphere.

Needs for Further Research

A study reviewed by Peter Griffin (2018) confirms wherever English went-Canada, the U.S., Australia, New Zealand- destroyed native languages, but in India, tribal communities continued to speak their languages, as did mainland Indians. Had the tribal languages of India given strength to the developed languages as well? This has also prompted to question. "Is there something in these languages that kept them strong, and kept their communities undestroyed and non-colonised. For hundreds of communities, economic development is hampered when their language is denied official existence with no school lessons in their tongues, they lag behind their peers. Later their employability and incomes remain low. In an alarming finding, UNESCO's Atlas of the World's Languages in Danger had already listed 180 Indian languages. After Independence, India continued to change with linguistic states being adopted, even some major languages became marginal. Is it not natural that languages evolve, die, as they have done for thousands of years? But when a language dies, something irreplaceable dies. Researches have to understand how languages get pushed to the edge for other reasons. The normally cited reasons are lack of political patronage, policy inadequacy, the language does not get taught due to non- recognition, non-availability of employment in the language.

References

Agarwal, P. (2006). *Higher Education in India: The Need for Change*. (Report). Retrieved from http://latrobe.summon.serials solutions.com

Anandakrishnana, (2018). Response of Higher Education to Emerging Challenges of the Future, *University news*, 56 (12) March 19-25.

Annamalai, K., & Rao, S. (2003). *What works:ITC'S E-CHOUPAL and Profitable Rural Transformation*. Michigan: University of Michigan. Retrieved from http://pdf.wri.org/dd_echoupal.pdf

Auletta, K. (2012 . 08/10/2012). Why India's Newspaper Industry is Thriving. *The New Yorker*

Condé Nast. Retrieved from http://www.newyorker.com/reporting/ 2012/10/08/121008fa_fact_auletta

Australian Bureau of Statistics. (2010). *QuickStats* Retrieved 11/5/2010, 2010, from http://www.abs.gov.au/websitedbs/ censushome.nsf/ home/quickstats?opendocument & navpos=220

Bailey, R. W., & Görlach, M. (1983). *English as a World Language*: University of Michigan Press.

Baldridge, J. (2002). *Languages in India, Strength for Today and Bright Hope for Tomorrow. Strength for Today and Bright Hope for Tomorrow*. Retrieved 28.01.2009, 2009, from http:// www.language inindia.com/junjul2002/baldridgeindianenglish .html

Basu, K. (2007). India's Demographic Dividend. *BBC*. BBC. Retrieved from http://newsvote.bbc.co.uk/mpapps/pagetools/ print/ news.bbc.co.uk/2/hi/south_asia/6911544.stm

BBC. (2013). *Languages of the world*. Retrieved 15/6/2013, 2013, from http://www.bbc.co.uk/languages/guide/languages.shtml

Beck, U., & Camiller, P. (2000). *What is globalization?* Malden, MA: Polity Press.

Beldarrain, Y. (2006). Distance Education Trends: Integrating New Technologies to Foster Student Interaction and Collaboration. *Distance Education, 27*(2), 139-153.

Berry, J. W. (2008, 7//). Globalisation and acculturation. *International Journal of Intercultural Relations, 32*(4), 328-336. doi:http:/ / dx.doi.org/10.1016/j.ijintrel.2008.04.001

Bisong, J. (1995). Language choice and cultural imperialism: A Nigerian perspectives. *ELT Journal, 49*, 122-167.

Biswas, S. (2006). India warning on globalisation. *BBC*. BBC. Retrieved from http://news.bbc.co.uk/2/hi/south_asia/ 6195617.stm

Biswas, S. (2011, 31/03/2011). India's census: The good and bad news.*BBC*. BBC.

Bolton, K., Graddol, D., & Mesthrie, R. (2008, 03/2008). English Yesterday and Today. *English Today, 24*(01), 2.

Brewer, J., & Hunter, A. (1989). *Multimethod Research: A Synthesis of Styles*: Sage Publications.

British Association for Applied Linguistics (Ed.). (1996). *Change* and Language: Papers from the Annual Meeting of the British Association for Applied Linguistics Held at the University of *Leeds, September 1994*: British Association for Applied Linguistics, in association with Multilingual Matters. Retrieved from http://books.google.com.au/ books?id=3382tteyMXUC

British Council. (2008). *The English language*. Retrieved 05/02/2008, 2008, from http://www.britishcouncil.org/learning-faq-theenglish- language.htm

British Council. (2013). *The English language*. Retrieved 05/7/2013, 2013, from http://www.britishcouncil.org/learning-faq-theenglish- language.htm

Brown, R. (2010). *The British Empire in India* (Political Science, Ashland University, Grove City, Ohio). Retrieved from http:// www.ashbrook.org/publicat/thesis/brown/brown.pdf

Brutt-Griffler, J. (1998). Conceptual Questions in English as a World Language. *World Englishes, 17*, 381-392.

Brutt-Griffler, J. (2002). *World English: A Study of Its Development*. Clevedon: Multilingual Matters.

Bulard, M. (2007). *India's Boundless Ambitions*. Retrieved 5/2/2010, 2010, from http://mondediplo.com/2007/01/02india

Burton, A. M. (1998). *At the Heart of the Empire: Indians and the Colonial Encounter in Late-Victorian Britain*. Berkeley: University of California Press.

Canagarajah, A. S. (2005). *Reclaiming the Local in Language Policy and Practice*: Lawrence Erlbaum Assoc Incorporated.

Canagarajah, S. (2006). Changing Communicative Needs, Revised Assessment Objectives: Testing English as an International Language. *Language Assessment Quarterly, 3*(3), 229-242.

ChanLin, L.-J., Hong, J.-C., Horng, J.-S., Chang, S.-H., & Hui-Chuan,

C. (2006). Factors Influencing Technology Integration in Teaching: a Taiwanese Perspective. *Innovations in Education and Teaching International, 43* (1), 57-68.

Chew, P. G. L. (1999). Linguistic imperialism, globalism and the English language. *AILA Review, 13*(37-47).

Clackson, J., Horrocks, G., & Library, E. B. L. e. (2011). *The Blackwell History of the Latin Language*. Chicester: John Wiley & Sons.

Cogo, A., & Jenkins, J. (2010). English as a lingua Franca in Europe: A Miss Match Between Policy and Practice. *European Journal of Langyage Policy, 2* (2), 271-293.

Coleman, H. (2011). The English Language in Development. *MEXTESOL, 35*(1).

Connor, U., Davis, K. W., Rycker, T. D., Phillips, E. M., & Verckens, J. P. (1997). An International Course in International Business Writing: Belgium, Finland, the United States. *Business Communication Quarterly, 60*(4), 63-74.

Creswell, J. W. (1998). *Qualitative Inquiry and Research Design: Choosing Among Five Traditions*. Thousand Oaks: Sage Publications.

Creswell, J. W. (2003). *Research Design: Qualitative, Quantitative, and Mixed Method Approaches*: Sage Publications.

Creswell, J. W. (2003). *Research Design: Qualitative, Quantitative, and Mixed Method Approaches*. Thousand Oaks, Calif: Sage Publications.

Crotty, M. (1998). *The foundations of Social Research: Meaning and Perspective in the Research Process*. St Leonards, NSW: Allen & Unwin.

Crystal, D. (1997). *English as a Global Language*. Cambridge: Cambridge University Press.

Crystal, D. (2001). *Language and the Internet*. Cambridge: Cambridge University press.

Crystal, D. (2003). *English as a Global Language*. Cambridge: Cambridge University Press.

Crystal, D. (2004). *Subcontinent Raises its Voice*. Retrieved 06/12/ 2006, 2006, from http://www.guardian.co.uk/education/2004/nov/19/tefl

Crystal, D. (2005). *Mother Tongue India*. Retrieved 06/12/2006, 2006, from http://www.guardian.co.uk/education/2004/nov/19/tefl

Crystal, D. (2006). *Language and the Internet*: Cambridge University Press.

Daniel, A. (2007). *Languages in India*. Retrieved 05/01/2007, 2007, from http://adaniel.tripod.com/aharonbio.htm

Dasgupta, J. (1970). *Language Conflict and National Development: Group Politics and National Language Policy in India*. Berkeley: University of California Press.

Davidson, K. (2007). The nature and significance of English as a Global Language. *English Today, 23*(01), 48-50.

Deterding, D. (2011). Indian English by Pingali Sailaja. *Journal of Sociolinguistics, 15*(3), 412-415.

Denzin, N. K., & Lincoln, Y. S. (Eds.). (1994). *Handbook of Qualitative Research*. Thousand Oaks: Sage Publications.

Dossani, R. (2003). *Doing Business in India: Issues in Software and Business Process Offshoring*. Retrieved 02/05, 2011, from http:/ / asia.stanford.edu/events/fall03/ slides/dossaniSlides.pdf

Drucker, P. (2006). *Josh Marshall Excerpts an Interview with Peter*

Drucker. Retrieved 08/12/2006, 2006, from <http:// www.talkingpointsmemo.com/ archives/002366.html>

Editorial (2018). Special Issue on Innovation Entrepreneurship and Disruptive Technology in Higher Education, University News, 56(12) March 19-25, 2018.

English Language Guide. (2013). *English Language Statistics*. Retrieved 6/7/2013, 2013, from http://www.english language guide.com/facts/stats/

Firth, A. (1996). The Discursive Accomplishment of Normality. On 'Lingua Franca' English and Conversation Analysis. *Journal of Pragmatics, 26*, 237-259.

Fishman, J. A. (1987). The Spread of English. *World Englishes, 6*(2), 169-170. doi:10.1111/j.1467-971X.1987.tb00192.x

Fraenkel, J. R., & Wallen, N. E. (1996). *How to Design and Evaluate Research in Education*. New York: McGraw-Hill.

Friesen, N., & Anderson, T. (2004). Interaction for Lifelong Learning. *British Journal of Educational Technology, 35*(6), 679-687. doi:10.1111/j.1467-8535.2004.00426.x

Gay, L. R. (1996). *Educational research*. New Jersey: Prentice Hall, Inc.

Gay, L. R. (1996). *Educational research: Competencies for Analysis and Application* (5 ed.). Englewood Cliffs, NJ: : Prentice-Hall.

Government of India. (2003). *India Tourism Statistics 2003*. Delhi: Ministry of Tourism

Retrieved from http://tourism.gov.in/statistics/FTAIS2003.pdf Government of India. (2007). *Working Group on Languages* & Book

Promotion: G. O. I. Planning Commission. (5). Retrieved from http:/ / planningcommission.nic.in/plans/planrel/11thf.htm

Gnanakan,K., Sam Daniel, Jonothan Lembright,(2007). *Education and Mission Internation Council for Higher Education*, Theological Book Trust, Bangalore.

Graddol, D. (1996, 1997). *The Future of English? : a Guide to* Forecasting the Popularity of the English Language in the 21st *Century*. London.

Graddol, D. (1997). *The Future of English?: A Guide to Forecasting the Popularity of the English Language in the 21st Century*. London: British Council.

Graddol, D. (2006). *English Next: Why Global English May Mean the End of 'English as a Foreign Language'*. London: British Council. Retrieved from http:// www.britishcouncil.org/learningresearch- englishnext.htmz

Graddol, D. (2010). *English Next India: The Future of English in India*: British Council.

Guba, E. G., & Lincoln, Y. S. (1988). The Countenances of Fourth Generation Evaluation: Description, Judgment and Negotiation. *Evaluation Studies Review Annual, NO. 11,*, 70-78.

Gubrium, J. F., & Holstein, J. A. (1997). *The New Language of Qualitative Method.* New York: Oxford University Press.

Haegeman, P. (2002). Foreigner Talk in Lingua Franca Business Telephone Calls. In K. Knapp & C. Meierkord (Eds.), *Lingual Franca Communication*. Frankfurt am Main, Germany: Peter Lang.

Hamel, J., Dufour, S., & Fortin, D. (1993). *Case Study Methods.* Newbury Park,CA: Sage Publications.

Hayden, M. E. (2012 September 2012). *In India, English-Language Newspapers Are Thriving.* Retrieved 2013, 07/03/2013, from http:/ /adage.com/article/global-news/india-english-language-newspapersthriving/ 237795/

Hellstein, M., & Reid, A. M. (Eds.). (2008). *Researching International* Pedagogies: Sustainable Practice for Teaching and Learning in *Higher Education*. Dordrecht: Springer. Retrieved from http:/ / www.springer.com/education+%26+language/ higher+education/ book/978-1-4020-8857-5

Hogg, R. M., & Denison, D. (2006). *A History of the English Language*. Cambridge, UK ; New York: Cambridge, UK ; New York : Cambridge University Press.

Hohenthal, A. (2003). English in India, Loyalty and Attitudes. *Language in India, 3*(1). Retrieved from http:// www.languageinindia.com/ index.html

House, J. (1999). Misunderstanding in Intercultural Communication: Interactions in English as a Lingua Franca and the Myth of Mutual Intelligibility. In C. Gnutzmann (Ed.), *Teaching and Learning English as a Global Language* (pp. 73–89). Germany: Stauffenburg.: Tübingen,.

House, J. (2003). English as a Lingua Franca: A Threat to Multilingualism? *Journal of Sociolinguistics, 7*(4), 556-578. ·

India Online. (2009, 04/2009). *India Online 2009 Main Report*. New Delhi: J. Consult. (12/6/2010). Retrieved from http://www.juxt consult. com/Reports/Juxt_India _ Online_2009_ Main_Report.pdf -206- indiastat.com. (2012). *Revealing India Statistically*. Retrieved 05/ 05/ 2012, from http://www.indiastat.com. ezproxy.lib. monash.edu.au/education/6370/stats.aspx indiastat.com. (2013). *Revealing India Statistically*. Retrieved 05/ 05/ 2013, from http://www.indiastat.com. ezproxy.lib. monash.edu.au/default.aspx indiastat.com. (2018). *Revealing India Statistically*. Retrieved 22/ 03/ 2018, from http://www.indiastat.com. ezproxy.lib. monash.edu.au/default.aspx

Jasuja, L., Kashyap, Prashant (2007). Vocational Education in India: Key Challenges & New Directions. Retrieved 2011, from http:/ / www.technopak.com/ Perspective/vol3/Vocational%20 Education% 20In%20 India%20Key%20 Challenges% 20 and %20 New% 20 Directions.pdf

Jenkins, J. (2000). *The Phonology of English as an International Language*. Oxford, UK: Oxford University Press.

Jenkins, J. (2002). A Sociolinguistically Based, Empirically Researched Pronunciation Syllabus for English as an International Language. *Applied Linguistics, 23*, 83-103.

Jenkins, J. (2004). Research in Teaching Pronunciation and Intonation. *Annual Review of Applied Linguistics, 24*, 109-125.

Jenkins, J. (2009). English as a Lingua Franca: Interpretations and Attitudes. *World Englishes, 28*(2), 200-207.

Kachru, B. B. (1983). *The Indianization of English : the English language in India*. Delhi ; New York: Oxford.

Kachru, B. B. (1985). Standards, Codification and Sociolinguistic Realism: The English Language in the Outer Circle. In R. Quirk & H. G. Widdowson (Eds.), *English in the World* (pp. 11-30). Cambridge: Cambridge University Press.

Kachru, B. B. (2001). World Englishes and Culture War. In C. K. Tong & E. Thumboo (Eds.), *Ariels: Departures & Returns : Essays for Edwin Thumboo*: Oxford University Press.

Kachru, B. B., Kachru, Y., & Nelson, C. L. (2006). *The Handbook of World Englishes*. Malden, MA: Blackwell Pub.

Kankaanranta, A. (2006). "Hej Seppo, Could You Pls Comment on This!"—Internal Email Communication in Lingua Franca English in a Multinational Company. *Business Communication Quarterly, 69*(2), 216-225.

Kankaanranta, A., & Louhiala-Salminen, L. (2007). Business Communication in BELF. *Business Communication Quarterly, 70*(1), 55-59.

Kasper, G. (1984). Pragmatic Comprehension in Learner Native Speaker Discourse. *Language Learning, 34*(4), 1-20. doi:10.1111/j.1467- 1770.1984.tb00349.x

Kaur, J. (2011). Intercultural Communication in English as a Lingua Franca: Some Sources of Misunderstanding. *Intercultural Pragmatics, 8*(1), 93-116.

Kearney, A. T. (2008, 24/ 07/ 2008). *Location Roadmap for it- BPO Growth: Assessment of 50 leading cities*. Retrieved 21/04, 2011, from http://www.nasscom.in/Nasscom/templates/NormalPage. aspx?id=53873

Khanna, N. (2007, Oct-Dec 2007). Will India be a Superpower by 2020. *IIITA's e-Magazine, 4*(15).

Khokhar, R. (2006). *English in India?* Retrieved 2006, from http://www.chillibreeze.com/EnglishinIndia.asp

Kirkpatrick, A. (2010). English as an Asian Lingua Franca and the Multilingual Model of ELT. *Language Teaching, 44*(02), 212-224.

Knapp, K., & Meierkord, C. (2002). Approaching Lingua Franca Communication. In K. Knapp & C. Meierkord (Eds.), *Lingua Franca Communication* (pp. 9-28). Frankfurt am Main, Germany: Peter Lang.

Korpela, J. Y. (2003). English - The Universal Language on the Internet? *Human Languages*. Retrieved from http://www.cs.tut.fi/ ~jkorpela/ lingua-franca.html

Krishnasamy, K. (2007). English in Tamil: The Language of Advertising. *English Today,, 23*(3-4), 40-49.

Languages Spoken in India. (2013). [Image]. India: *Turret Tours & Travels*. Retrieved 27/05/2013, from http://www.turrettours.com/ languages_spoken_in_india.php

Lesznyák, Á. (2002). From Chaos to the Smallest Common Denominator. Topic Management in English Lingua Franca Communication. In K. Knapp & C.

Meierkord (Eds.), *Lingual Franca Communication*. Frankfurt am Main, Germany: Peter Lang.

Lewis, M. P. e. (Ed.). (2009). *Ethnologue: Languages of the World* (16 ed.). Dallas, Tex: SIL International. Online version: http:/ / www.ethnologue.com/.

Little, D. (2011). The Common European Framework of Reference for Languages: A Research Agenda. *Language Teaching, 44*(3), 381- 393. doi:10.1017/ S0261444811000097

Louhiala-Salminen, L., Charles, M., & Kankaanranta, A. (2005a). English as a Lingua Franca in Nordic Corporate Mergers: Two Case Companies. *English for Specific Purposes, 24*, 401-421.

Louhiala-Salminen, L., Charles, M., & Kankaanranta, A. (2005b). English as a Lingua Franca in Nordic Corporate Mergers: Two Case Companies. *English for Specific Purposes, 24*(4), 401-421. doi:10.1016/j.esp.2005.02.003

Macaulay, T. B. (1835). *Minute on Indian Education. Bureau of* Education. Selections from Educational Records, Part I (1781- *1839).* . Retrieved 2/5/2011, 2011, from http:// www.columbia.edu/ itc/mealac/pritchett/00generallinks/ macaulay/ txt_minute_education_1835.html

Martin, H. (2013). *Six Global Trends Shaping the Business World- Emerging Markets Increase their Global Power*. Retrieved 6/ 05/2013, from http://www.ey.com/ GL/en/Issues/Businessenvironment/ Six-global-trends-shaping-the-business-world— Emerging-markets-increase-their-global-power

Masani, Z. (2012). English or Hinglish - Which Will India Choose. *BBC News Magazine*. Retrieved from http://www.bbc.co.uk/ news/ magazine-20500312

Mesthrie, R. (2008). Sociolinguistics and Sociology of Language. In B. Spolsky & F. M. Hult (Eds.), *The Handbook of Educational Linguistics*.

Maykut, P. S., & Morehouse, R. (1994). *Beginning Qualitative Research: A Philosophic and Practical Guide*. London: Falmer Press.

McArthurr, T. (2003, April, 2003). English as an Asian Language. *English Today, 19, 2*(74).

Mehta, A. P., & Mehta, R. (2012). Internet Based Education in India Paradigm in Contemporary Learning. *Indian Journal of Research, 1*(12), 146-147.

Meierkord, C. (2002). 'Language Stripped Bare' or 'Linguistic Masala'? Culture in Lingua Franca Conversation. In K. Knapp & C. Meierkord (Eds.), *Lingual Franca Communication*. Frankfurt am Main, Germany: Peter Lang.

Melchers, G., & Shaw, P. (2003). *World Englishes*. London: Arnold. Merriam, S. B. (1998).

Qualitative Research and Case Study Applications in *Education*. San Francisco: Jossey-Bass Publishers.

Meredith, R., & Hoppough, S. (2016). Why Globalization is Good. Retrieved from https://www.forbes.com/free_forbes/2007/0416/064.html

Mertens, D. M. (1998). *Research Methods in Education and* Psychology: Integrating Diversity with Quantitative & *Qualitative Approach*. Thousand Oaks: Sage Publications.

Mesthrie, R. (2008, March 2008). English Circling the Globe. *English Today, 24*(01), 28-32.

Miller, J. (1999). *Speaking English and Social Identity: Migrant Students in Queensland High School* (PhD Thesis, University of Queensland, Brisbane, Australia).

Minichiello, V., Aroni, R., & Hays, T. (2008). *In-depth Interviewing: Principles, Techniques, Analysis*. Sydney: Pearson Education Australia.

Mirjaliisa, C. (1996). Business Negotiations: Interdependence Between Discourse and the Business Relationship. *English for Specific Purposes, 15*(1), 19-36.

Mishra, P. (2006). *The Western View of the Rise of India and China is a Self-affirming Fiction.* Retrieved 08/07/2008, 2008, from http:/ /www.gua rdia n. co.u k/ comment i s f r ee/ 20 06 / jun/1 0/ comment.china

Molly Easo Smith, (2018). The Imperative to Globalize : Forging Connection between US and Indian Institutions of Higher Education, *University News,* 56 (12) March 15-23.

Montaut, A. (2010). English in India and the Role of the Elite in the National Project. In S. I. Hasnain & S. Chaudhary (Eds.), Problematizing Language Studies, Cultural, Theoretical and Applied Perspectives, Essays in Honor of Rama Kant Agnihotri. (pp. 83- 116). Delhi: Akar Books,.

Mukherjee, P. (2010). *India Budget speech:Transcript:*. Retrieved 23/ 07/2011, 2011, from http://www.ft.com/cms/s/0/373895 .html

Mutur Zikin. (2011). *List of Languages of the World by Name.* Retrieved 06/05/ 2013, 2013, from http://www.muturzikin.com/ languages.htm

Narayan, R. K. (2006). *My days: Autobiography*: Indian Thought Publications.

National Network of Education (NNE). (2011). *National Policy on Education.* Retrieved 05/06/2012, 2012, from http:// www.indiaeducat ion.net / india edudest inat ion/policy/ education_policy.asp

Nation Master. (2012). *Language Statistics*. Retrieved 05/05/2012,

2012, from http://www.nationmaster.com/red/pie/lan_eng_spelanguage- english-speakers

Nayak, S. (2002). *Language of Advertisements in Tamil Mass Media* (Linguistic, University of Mysore, Mysore). Retrieved from http:/ / www.languageinindia. com/may2002/sandhyathesis.html

Nelson, C., Treichler, P. A., & Grossberg, L. (1992). Cultural Studies: An Introduction. In L. Grossberg, C. Nelson & P. A. Treichler (Eds.), *Cultural Studies* (pp. 1-16). New York: Routledge.

Nickerson, C. (2005). English as a L*ingua Franca* in International Business Contexts. *English for Specific Purposes, 24*(4), 367-380.

Observer Review. (2003, 26 August 2003). *Murdoch and China*. Retrieved 02/05, 2010, from http://www.guardian.co.uk/media/ 2003/aug/24/chinathemedia. rupertmurdoch

One India. (2008, 5/5/2008). *NASSCOM-A.T KEARNEY Study on* 50 *cities for IT-BPO Growth.* . Retrieved 4/6/2010, 2010, from http:// news.oneindia.in/2008/ 05/05/nasscom-at-kearney-study-on-50-cities-forit-bpo-growth-1209978174.html

Ostler, N. (2010). *The Last Lingua Franca: English Until the Return of Babel*: Penguin Books Limited.

Park, J. S.-Y., & Wee, L. (2011). A Practice Based Critique of English as a Lingua Franca. *World Englishes, 30*(3), 360-374.

Patton, M. Q. (2002). *Qualitative Research and Evaluation Methods*: Sage Publications.

Paul, D. (2012). What's the Most Difficult Language? *DP English Services*. Retrieved 14/12/2012, from http:// www.dougpaulo.com/ my-last-posts Pennycook, A. (1994). *The Cultural Politics of English as an International Language*. London: Longman.

Phillipson, R. (2001). English for Globalisation or for the World's People? *International Review of Education, 47*(3-4), 185-200

Provenzo, E. F. J. (1999). *The Internet and the World Wide Web for Preservice Teachers*. Boston: Allyn & Bacon.

Quirk, R. (1968). *The Use of English*. New York St. Martin's Press. Rajesh Tandon, Higher Education in India Tomorrow, World Class and Socially Responsible, University News, 56 (12) March 19-25, 2018.

Rajan, S. I., Sarma, P. S., & Mishra, U. S. (2003). Demography of Indian Aging, 2001-2051. *Journal of Aging & Social Policy, 15*(2- 3), 11-30. doi:10.1300/ J031v15n02_02

Rakshit, P. (2009). *The Nielsen Upper Middle and Rich (UMAR) survey* Retrieved 03/11/2010 2009 from http://www.afaqs.com/ news/story/ 24852_Nielsen-study-says-rich-Indians-prefer-Englishnewspapers- Hindi-TV-programs

Reeves-Ellington, R., & Library, E. B. L. e. (2010). *What is Culture?: Generating and Applying Cultural Knowledge*. Lewiston: Edwin Mellen Press.

Riddick, J. F. (2006). *The History of British India: A Chronology*: Praeger.

Rogerson-Revell, P. (2007). *English Phonology and Pronunciation Teaching*: Continuum International Publishing Group.

Ruellot, V. (2011). English in French Print Advertising from 1999 to 2007. *World Englishes, 30*(1), 5-20.

Sailaja, P. (2009). *Indian English*. Edinburgh: Edinburgh University Press.

Samata, P. (2012). Importance of Effective Communication skills.*Language In India, 12*(10), 333.

Sarma, S.S. (2012). 'Osum' Shakespeare and the 'Mincemeat of English. *The Hindu*. The Hindu. Retrieved from http:// www.thehindu.com/ opinion/open-page/ article3315382.ece

Sarma, S.S. (2012, 15/04/2012). 'Osum' Shakespeare and the 'Mincemeat of English. *The Hindu*. Kasturi and Sons Limited. Retrieved from http://www.thehindu.com/ opinion/open-page/ osum-s ha kes p ea r e- a nd- t he-minc emea t -of - engl i s h/ article3315382.ece

Sarwal, A. (2004, November 17, 2004). *Emergence of English as a World Language. SEARCHWARP.COM*. Retrieved 12/01/2008, 2008, from http://searchwarp.com/ swa3682.htm

Sarwal, A. (2011). *Emergence of English as a World Language:The Need for a Global Link Language*. Retrieved 25/06/2011, 2011, from http://www.religiousunity.or g/NewsArt/English% 20as%20a%20World%20Language.html#_ftn1

Schneider, E. W. (2003). The Dynamics of New Englishes: From Identity Construction to Dialect Birth. *Linguistic Society of America, 79*(2), 233-281.

Sedlatschek, A. (2009). *Contemporary Indian English: Variation and Change*. Amsterdam ; Philadelphia :: John Benjamins Pub.Co. .

Seidlhofer, B. (2001). Closing a Conceptual Gap: The Case for a Description of English as a Lingua Franca. *International Journal of Applied Linguistics, 11*(2), 133-158.

Seidlhofer, B. (2004). Research Perspectives on Teaching English as a Lingua Franca. *Annual Review of Applied Linguistics, 24*, 209-239.

Seidlhofer, B. (2009). Common Ground and Different Realities: World Englishes and English as a Lingua Franca. *World Englishes, 28*(2), 236-245.

Sharma,P.B., (2018). Presidential Address, Higher Education in India : Focus on Values, Relevance and Creadivity, *University News*,56 (12) March 19-25.

Shilling, A. G. (2012, 17/12/2012). *Why India Will Displace China as Global Growth Engine*. Retrieved 25/7/2013, 2013, from http://www.bloomberg.com/news/2012-12-16/why-india-willdisplace- china-as-global-growth-engine.html

Smith, R. (1997). *English in Current European Spanish*. Retrieved 08/ 07/2009, 2009, from http://www.telefonica.net/web2/ rossko/ ENGINSPAN.html

Sood, K. (1988). *Evolution of International Trade in South Asia: India, Pakistan and Bangladesh*: Institut Universitaire de Hautes Etudes Internationales.

Stake, R. (1995). *The Art of Case Research*. . Thousand Oaks, CA: Sage Publications.

Stanley, S. (1939). British Imperialism in India: A Chart of the Exploitation of 375,000,000 People. *New International, 5*(10), 308-310.

Tashakkori, A., & Teddlie, C. (2003). *Handbook of Mixed Methods in Social & Behavioral Research*: Sage Publications.

Teclehaimanot, B., & Hickman, T. (2011). Student Teacher Interaction on Facebook: What Students Find Appropriate. *TechTrends, 55*(3), 19-0 The Economist. (2013, 30/03/2013). Can India Become a Great Power? *The Economist, , 2013*(06/05/2013). Retrieved from http:// www.economist.com/news/leaders/21574511-indias- 216- lack-strategic- culture-hobbles-its-ambition-be-force-world-canindia

The Times. (2010). *Times Higher Education's Annual World University Rankings*. Retrieved 02/03, 2011, from http://www.times higher education.co.uk/world-university-rankings/

The Times of India. (11 Nov 2005). *India is the 2nd Largest English Speaking Nation*. Retrieved 08/04/2010, 2010, from http:// articles.timesofindia.indiatimes.com/2005-11-11/education/ 27840263_1_american-english-foreign-language-largestenglish- speaking-nation

Thomex.com. (2011, May 26, 2011). *New Roadmap for India's Growth*. Retrieved May 26, , 2011, from http:// www.thomex.com/article/ resources_details.aspx?id=r_20070604141746

Trudgill, P. (2006). Standard English: What It Isn't. Retrieved 23/ 11/ 2012, 2011, from http://www.phon.ucl.ac.uk/home/dick/ SEtrudgill.htm

Trudgill, P., & Hannah, J. (1994). International English: A Guide to Varieties of Standard English: E. Arnold.

Verma, S. K., & Krishnaswamy, N. (1989). Modern Linguistics: An Introduction. Delhi:: Oxford University Press.

Vrasidas, C., & Zembylas, M. (2003). The Nature of Technology-Mediated Interaction in globalized Distance Education. International Journal of Training and Development, 7(4), 271- 286. doi:10.1046/ j.1360-3736.2003.00186.

Warsi, M. J. (2008). Linguistic Dynamism In South Asia: Gyan Publishing House.

Westera, W. (2011). On the Changing Nature of Learning Context: Anticipating the Virtual Extensions of the World.. Educational Technology & Society, 14 (2), 201–212.

Williams, J. (2005). Teaching Writing in Second and Foreign Language Classrooms. New York : McGraw-Hill.

Yin, R. K. (2003). Case Study Research: Design and Methods: Sage Publications.

Index

O

P

R

S

T

U

V

W

Y